PARADOX OF POWER:

Balancing Personal and Higher Will

by
Mark Thurston, Ph.D.

A.R.E.® PRESS • VIRGINIA BEACH • VIRGINIA

OTHER BOOKS BY MARK THURSTON

The Inner Power of Silence
Discovering Your Soul's Purpose
Edgar Cayce's Predictions for the New Age
Experiments in Practical Spirituality
How to Interpret Your Dreams
Understand and Develop Your ESP
Experiments in a Search for God
Meditation and the Mind of Man (co-author)

ISBN 87604-208-6

Printed in the U.S.A.

CONTENTS

CONTENTS

PART TWO:
Training and Using Your Will

CONTENTS

and a specific technique. Small group work, group consciousness, and "pooled will." Self-observation done with nonjudgmental objectivity. Disciplines countering habits; disciplines which are somewhat artificial but allow the will to focus and change a habit pattern. Loving self-assertion that affirms one's own real individuality. Staying in the now, resisting the temptation to overplan the future or to try to change the past. Four exercises derived from Steiner's suggestions for educating the will of a child. Imitation by which we learn how to manifest a healthy will. Building rhythms into life. Letting go of some mechanized, labor-saving devices that put the will to sleep. Moving the limbs of the body purposefully. Setting a reachable daily goal. Choosing a spiritual ideal.

Decision-making styles. Two forms of guidance. Three guidance strategies: (1) Looking for an answer. The limitations of esoteric arts like astrology. (2) Looking for more information. (3) Looking for confirmation or warning. The paradox of effective decision making. Realms #1 and #2 of will. Parallels between the soul's mission and realm #1 will. James on making hard decisions. Healthy will development begins by recognizing two domains. The typical, human way of decision making which ignores realm #1 will. Two ways that realm #1 will can help to guide us: imagination and synchronicity. A nine-step decision-making procedure which respects both realms of your will.

PART THREE:
Living Your Life with Good Will

The purposes and limitations of a model. The essential opposition of mind and will. Orthogonal opposition—two intersecting, perpendicular axes—is the best way to depict

CONTENTS

it. An illustration of the creation story or the model. The same story depicted in the fairy tale *Pinocchio*. The meaning of "Ameliorate" and "Amelius" in the creation story. Parallel ideas from Rudolf Steiner. How to understand our current human state in terms of mind and will. The nature of the Path or intended plan for our spiritual evolution. A descending arc on the model: a period of limited mind expansion but definite will development. Where are you on the model? The ideal state on the model.

Our contemporary problem with evil. Will is at the heart of the problem with the power of evil. Peck's three models of good and evil: non-dualism, integrated dualism, and diabolical dualism. A deeper exploration of integrated dualism. Evil is good gone wrong. Two faces of evil as described by Martin Buber. The examples of sexuality and money making. Parallel ideas from Steiner about the two faces of evil: Lucifer and Ahriman. The Christ as an integrative, balance point between the two extremes. The nature of evil depicted on the model from Chapter 5. Will and evil in the legend of *Faust* by Goethe. The role of will in the world of good and evil. The ideal of good will. A new age as an "Age of Good Will."

Why develop the will? Intentionality and ideals. Three levels of an ideal: the spiritual ideal, the incarnation ideal, the conscious ideal. Five steps in a personal research project to find your life's mission: (1) Set your ideal. (2) Identify your soul's talents. (3) Formulate a mission theme. (4) List applications of the mission theme. (5) Test the applications in real life. An example of the research project in the life of one woman. The role of the will in finding and living your personal destiny.

ACKNOWLEDGMENTS

I wish to thank those individuals who helped to shape the ideas in this book. Foremost, of course, are the many creative thinkers and writers whose books and articles are listed in the Recommended Additional Reading sections at the end of each chapter. The questions of free will, freedom, and power are ancient ones, and any contemporary contribution to these issues must honor and appreciate what has come before.

Then, there were the friends and colleagues who shared their ideas and gave insightful critiques of their own. Among those in this group are my wife Mary, David Aberegg, Robert Witt, Rudolf Wilhelm, Eleanor Beckham, and Jacob Needleman.

Finally, I want to recognize a group of people who assisted me in the preparation and shaping of the manuscript. Valuable suggestions on early versions of the text were kindly provided by Richard Abrams, James Windsor, and Harmon Bro. Editorial support came from Elaine Hruska and Ruth Braun. Thank you all.

INTRODUCTION

Power. People crave it. The world respects it. Power is that elusive commodity that everyone promises, but no one seems quite to understand.

Power is the capacity to get things done. It is energy—sometimes pure and raw, sometimes purposefully directed. Horsepower, atomic power, the power of love.

Power means getting your way. Willpower, military power, people power.

Power is influence. It is a force that shapes, manipulates or controls. Political power, the power of suggestion, a higher, spiritual power.

But power is a paradox. It has two sides which seem to contradict each other. To have one kind of power, you must make the effort and work for it. But then, when you get it, you find it turns on itself. Power corrupts, and absolute power corrupts absolutely. You can easily become a slave to your personal power and end up truly powerless.

To have another kind of power, you must surrender. A higher, spiritual power can move through your life only if you don't try to grasp at it. Resurrection is possible only if there is first the release of crucifixion. To save your life you must be willing to lose your life.

How can any sense be made of all these contradictions? How can you work creatively and purposefully with power in your life when these paradoxes make understanding so difficult?

It isn't realistic to think that the mysterious contradictions can be explained away. Paradox is such a fundamental ingredient to the nature of power that we simply have to live with it. But it *is* possible to live in harmonious flow with contradictions of power. And the key to understanding how power acts in human life is the *will*. Not just willpower—that coercive, repressive force that is all too familiar. That may be one expression of will, one expression of power. But if willpower is all we feel of will and all we know of power, then our experience is pitifully limited.

Will is the key to understanding power. In human experience it is the spark that gives power its dynamic, living quality. But like power, the human will is a paradox.

There is, on the one hand, the strength and individual empowerment of will. A productive life is impossible without that kind of will. But it is never enough. We also need the complementary side of will—a higher will that is experienced only in moments of willing surrender.

This is a book about how to integrate two threads of life. One thread is making your own way. This means self-determination, free-willed choice, and personal responsibility. The second thread is following your destiny, being obedient to a higher plan, and living your soul's purpose. You can go wrong along the spiritual path if you act as if only one of these two threads is necessary. But as you shall discover in the chapters which follow, the seeker must harmonize the two aspects of will.

Part One of this book is a careful and in-depth exploration of the nature of will. What is it, how can we understand it, how do we know its living presence in life? What is the meaning of this key ingredient which brings power into our experience?

Part Two is a more practical examination of techniques related to the will. How can the will be awakened, trained, and made healthy? How can we make use of both sides of the will in order to make specific decisions in life?

Part Three asks the question, "What does it all mean?" One of these final three chapters addresses the essential problem of our world: the power of good and the power of evil. What role does the will play in creating or in counteracting the power of evil? Finally we shall discover that an awakened, healthy will makes possible the most empowering experience available to any individual—to discover and live what one was born to do, to fulfill one's destiny.

The paradox of power. No riddle is more important to the times in which we live. No enigma has been more misunderstood, and we have paid dearly for that misunderstanding—individually and collectively as a human family. Wars. Suppression. Frustrated lives. Power is something that we have rarely known how to use constructively and lovingly. But the heart of the problem rests with our ignorance of the human will. The mystery of power is the mystery of the willing spirit which lives within us.

PART ONE

What Is Your Will?

CHAPTER ONE

The Mystery of the Will

Your will is the greatest mystery of modern times. It is not the kind of mystery which is solved by playing detective and gathering facts. Instead, it is a deeper kind of mystery that rests in the very heart of your existence. If you experience the meaning and power of your will, then you know yourself in a whole new way.

Certainly there are other great mysteries. The human mind is one. Especially in the past 50 years there have been remarkable discoveries about the extraordinary realms of the unconscious mind. Research into meditation, hypnosis, dreams, and ESP has demonstrated previously unbelievable capacities of the mind. But it is the mystery of the will that should now gain our attention. All those tremendous features of the mind have meaning only if the will is healthy and alive—able to direct us properly.

What, in essence, is this mysterious principle we call the will? Even if we cannot fully explain it, we can still ask about the *qualities* it brings to living and about *how* it helps establish profound meaning in our lives.

The role of the will is among the most fundamental questions in contemporary spirituality. In many ways the so-called "consciousness movement" or "new religions" have failed to provide to people in our society what they have promised. Certainly the failure may be largely on the part of the people rather than the teachings.

On the one hand, we have an array of remarkable tools available to the contemporary seeker: insights and techniques ranging from meditation to reincarnation, from telepathy to biofeedback. Except for a few pockets of impressive change, why hasn't our culture been transformed? We have discovered the reality of psychosomatic health, the power of the mind to heal. Why are there so many sick people in our society? We have discovered the underlying oneness of all mind. Why is there still so much discord and animosity? We have discovered the inherent connections between human consciousness and the planet Earth. Why is there still pollution and disregard for the environment?

Perhaps what has been missing is a sensitive, honest encounter with this forgotten mystery of human experience: will. For all our scientific, psychological, and metaphysical achievements in the past two generations, we still seem to be rather powerless to bring about the kinds of changes in the world which are possible. The next great frontier for us is not in the realm of physical science, mental exploration, or philosophical speculation. The cutting edge of contemporary spirituality is our encounter with this profound mystery of the human will. If we become initiates of this mystery, it shall provide us with the inner power to achieve all of the possibilities for ourselves and for our world which we can envision, yet have seemed helplessly unable to manifest.

What is the will? Is it a particular state of mind? Is it a certain kind of energy? Or is it instead one of the basic building blocks of human experience, something on an equal footing with mind and energy itself? Perhaps the mystery and the power of the will is best understood by treating it as philosophers would a fundamental "category" of human life—that is to say, the will can be seen as something so basic to who we are that it cannot be explained in terms of other essential building blocks such as energy and mind.

By way of analogy, we might think of color. There are three primary pigments: red, blue, and yellow. These are the basic building blocks of other colors. The color green can be explained in terms of the interaction of two other primary colors: yellow and blue. The color purple, by the interaction of red and blue. But how can blueness be explained? It is not a specialized form of red or yellow, nor can it be created by a specialized mixing of these other two primary colors. Blue itself is one of the fundamental building blocks.

In a similar fashion, we can think of the will like a basic category of life, one of life's fundamental "colors." Will cannot be explained as a kind of energy nor as a particular state of mind. Life can be understood and given meaning only as we are able to see and relate to will as an independent faculty or ingredient of the soul on an equal footing with energy and mind.

We might go further and say that will is that which makes us nonmachine-like. We can never build a machine-like model of life that fully includes the impact of will because the will is not of that realm or order. Certainly, we can try to build models or analogies which help us understand how the will operates, but any such effort will have a limitation. The will introduces into human experience something that cannot be reduced to mechanistic formulas. If we were made up merely of energy and mind, then highly sophisticated flow charts might be able to account for all human experience. If we were made up of mind and energy alone, then we might foresee a time in the future when highly advanced computers could fully simulate human consciousness. But the will, as one of the three fundamental ingredients of the human soul (along with mind and life energy or spirit), makes machine-like replication impossible. In fact, there might be nothing more influential than current research in artificial intelligence to drive contemporary spiritual studies in the direction of appreciating the significance of the will.

A Historical Review

Today in our personal lives and in the world we face crises which can be traced back directly to a failure of the human will. Yet our inability to understand and appreciate the will is *not* due to the lack of efforts in history to study this problem. Despite an overall tendency to ignore or discount the will, there have always been those (from ancient times even to the present) who have made an effort to understand its power and significance. Despite the fact that a very influential segment of key modern thinkers in philosophy, psychology, and social and medical sciences still have no appreciation for the will, there is a long tradition about this topic. Over the centuries we see a sequence of questions and possible answers about the will being formulated, and it is this same sequence that each of us may go through in a personal encounter with the mystery and power of will.

The historical development of understanding centers around three questions, which can be posed first in philosophical language and then in more practical daily language.

1. Are we "free" or is life predestined?
2. What is it that connects thought and action?
3. Is there a faculty of the soul which stands opposite the impulses coming from the physical senses?

All three of these questions sound very intellectual, and yet they are questions which you may ask yourself in daily living in different forms. For example, you may find yourself wondering about the nature of freedom. To what extent is your life free? How much are you controlled by the patterns of living you learned from your parents and school teachers, or by the constraints placed upon you by the government and community in which you live? How much was your life predetermined at birth by your genetic makeup, which largely shaped your physical appearance and intelligence? Can you really say that you are free?

Or, why do you so often fail to do what you think you ought to do? Why do you often have the best of intentions and yet no physical actions or results come out of it? What are the mysterious connections that allow your thinking process to be translated into practical application?

Or, what keeps you from living your life totally by impulse? What keeps you from being merely a machine that *reacts* to life? What inward faculty allows you to choose and respond in your own best interest to physical stimuli and appetites? The answer to this and all of these questions rests with the nature of your will.

To study the way in which theologians, philosophers, and psychologists have for centuries wrestled with these kinds of questions leaves us with a difficulty in terminology. For example, we must ask whether or not ancient and modern thinkers used similar words to mean the same thing. Do terms such as "spirit," "will," and "reason" mean the same today that they meant hundreds of years ago? Furthermore, in any careful historical study, a whole array of related terms is also introduced—concepts such as wish, choice, purpose, impulse, appetite, and desire. In fact, another entire book would be required to summarize adequately the centuries of theories and argumentation on these questions about human experience. This book, however, is about a modern theory of the meaning of will and the paradoxical role it plays in a healthy experience of power.

Where do we begin in formulating a modern theory of the importance of the will? Some of the most influential thinkers of the 19th and 20th centuries don't provide support. For example, Charles Darwin and those evolutionists who followed him have little place for the human will in their theories. The principal agent of change in the development of humanity is not the will but, instead, genetic chemistry. Sigmund Freud in his psychoanalytic theories proposed that will is illusory, that the principal determining agent in our lives is a kind of primal impetus from the unconscious which he called the libido. Neither of these two great pillars of modern Western thought leave much room for a human faculty such as will.

One notable exception is the American philosopher and psychologist, William James, who wrote in the late 19th and early 20th centuries. James' ideas are a good starting point for a modern theory of will. His work has never been as popular as that of Freud, yet perhaps in the future he will be rediscovered and reappreciated. James went through long periods of extraordinary self-questioning—almost to the point of being self-destructive—concerning the question of personal freedom. Finally, he arrived at a conclusion (described in his diary on April 30, 1870) of *assuming* that free will *does* exist. For him, the first act of that free will was to assert its reality and to live life as if he had a self-determining agent within called will.

I think that yesterday was a crisis in my life. I finished the first part of Renouvier's second "essais" and see no reason why his definition of Free Will—"the sustaining of a thought *because I choose to* when I might have other thoughts"—need be the definition of an illusion. At any rate, I will assume for the present—

until next year—that it is no illusion. My first act of free will shall be to believe in free will.

Much of James' writing about the nature of will focuses on concerns about how it operates to create physical actions. How does the will help you move from the *idea* of doing something to the *act* of doing it? In his theory, the will draws upon the memory of previous physical movements. We are able to re-create voluntarily and freely physical movements because we can select memory patterns of the *sensations* created by those movements when they were completed in the past. You can choose to move your left arm because your will draws upon memories of how it felt in the past when you moved it. Of course, this notion creates a sort of "which came first, the chicken or the egg" dilemma. James proposed that any movement was *first* produced in a reflexive or accidental way and only then, by drawing upon the memory of it, could we voluntarily re-create actions with the will.

This principle of "Ideo-motor-action" and the related concept of "kinaesthetic image" make for a rather complicated theory that need not concern us here. What we do want to appreciate from William James' writings and come back to later are two key principles. First is the way in which the will is related to imagination. One of the ways in which we experience the workings of the will is through its capacity to function imaginatively. Your will can *activate* the imaginative function of your mind. It can stimulate imagination to draw upon memories of the feelings and sensations of the past. It works with body memories *and* the memories of thoughts and feelings. In other words, your will can direct the realm of your attitudes and emotions, if you use it. Through an act of will, you can create certain thoughts and feelings because you are able to draw imaginatively on memories of similar thoughts and feelings from the past.

There is a second key principle on which we can begin to build a modern theory of the will. James recognized that the fundamental faculty of the will is a capacity to *direct our attention.* The will allows us to put attention upon certain patterns of mind and not upon others. We have both an inner life and an outer life that go in particular directions fundamentally because the will can place attention on certain imaginings or mind patterns instead of upon others. If you wish to feel the reality of your own will *in this very moment*, experience the way in which you have the capacity to move your attention. Right now, put your attention on the color of this page of paper. Then move your attention to the top of your head. Finally move it to the memory of what you ate at your last meal. Your ability to do that simple, three-part exercise is evidence of your will in action.

We can build upon these two fundamental insights offered by James. Even though he was a pioneer in a modern appreciation for the human will, much more can be added. In Chapter 2 we will examine a broader picture of the nature of will. A new understanding is needed about this key ingredient which stands at the heart of our experience of power.

RECOMMENDED ADDITIONAL READING

"Will" in *The Great Ideas: A Syntopicon*, Volume 2, Mortimer Adler, editor (Encyclopedia Britannica, Inc., Chicago, 1952)

This extraodinarily rich essay appears as a chapter in the lengthy collection. It surveys the thinking of great philosophers about the nature of free will. Although it is not easy reading, it is highly recommended for anyone making a detailed study of the will, particularly the history of thought about this topic.

"Pelagius and Pelagianism" in *The New Catholic Encyclopedia*, Volume 11 (The Catholic University of America, Washington, D.C., 1967)

This essay summarizes a story that should be of interest to anyone concerned with the theological issue of free will. A debate in the 5th century focused on Pelagius' theory of the freedom of human will versus Augustine's theory of predestination.

"The Dilemma of Determinism" in *The Writings of William James*, John J. McDermott, editor (Random House, New York, 1967)

This essay is James' most fundamental philosophical statement about the human will. Also excerpted in this anthology is James' lengthy, detailed analysis of the will from a psychological viewpoint. That chapter is entitled merely "Will."

Love and Will, Rollo May (Norton, New York, 1969)

A leading, contemporary psychotherapist presents a detailed philosophical and clinical study of how these two qualities interact. This book is unusually deep for the popular best seller which it was. Of special significance are the four chapters which make up Part II, chapters directly dealing with the will.

CHAPTER TWO

A New Understanding of the Will

The time is ripe for a new understanding of the will. Of course, not everyone may agree, because some see no need for such a thing. For example, in modern psychology, where the behavioristic and psychoanalytic approaches predominate, there is no room for something like the will being a responsible director and shaper of our lives. But it is a hopeful sign that in the past two decades a developing new position in human psychology *does* appreciate the significance of the will. Many of the leading thinkers in both humanistic and transpersonal psychology have placed the will at the center of growth and development. In addition, the scientific study of biofeedback—i.e., the voluntary control of internal physical states—has begun to develop scientific credibility.

How can we move from these hopeful signs to a truly comprehensive picture of what the will is and what it can do in our lives? A good place to start is a multifaceted definition which shows the richness and the depth of meaning inherent in the human will. At least nine features should be a part of this new understanding. Each one is described in the extensive explanation of the will which is found in Edgar Cayce's psychic readings.

Active Principle. What can we call the will? Do we speak of it as a type of energy or as a state of mind? Or do we give the will equal status with pure energy as well as with the mind? To give the will that recognition, we need to select a label which stresses its independent status. Perhaps the best wording is the phrase "an *active principle* within the soul."

That is to say, it is a faculty inherent in the soul's nature. Furthermore, it is a principle which is *active*, which is dynamic and which participates in the soul's growth and evolution.

Let's make this abstract notion more practical. Suppose you suddenly remember that day after tomorrow is your uncle's birthday. Should you take the time and effort to send a card? What other obligations do you face today and how high a priority is it to keep your uncle happy? Suppose you decide to purchase and mail a card today. The remembrance of his birthday and the analysis of whether or not to send a card are both functions of your mind. But the decision in favor of sending a card and the behaviors needed to make that happen both fall in the realm of your will—an *active principle*.

Individualizer. The will is that which makes each of us an individual creation—it is that which makes each of us a *unique* spiritual being. If we use the concept that "mind is the builder," then in a complementary fashion we could say that "will is the individualizer."

But *how* is it that the will creates uniqueness and individuality? Is it analogous to the serial number on a television set or on the engine block of an automobile? No, because what makes us unique is not so much a specialized imprint as it is an active principle which allows us to be self-reflective or self-aware. The will is the individualizer because it allows us to know ourselves as ourselves. The hallmark of a being with a will is self-reflection.

Of course, we do not always live our lives with this kind of self-reflectiveness. Rarely do we take time to step outside ourselves and see ourselves objectively. For this reason, we can say that most often the will is asleep within us. It is unconscious—an untapped potential. But if the will awakens, then this kind of self-awareness leads to an awakening of true individuality.

Chooser. This is the faculty of will with which we are most familiar. The will allows us to make choices among alternative courses of action. However, the choosing process relates not just to physical behaviors but more fundamentally to the way in which we choose to direct attention. Recall that for William James this capacity to place attention in one direction instead of another is the fundamental way by which we experience the reality of will. Oftentimes our "choices" to act in certain ways are really quite predetermined by the way in which we have chosen to place our attention in the inner world of thought and feeling.

Agent of Obedience. Not only does the will allow each of us to chart a self-determined course for life, it also allows us to be subservient to or obedient to influences which come from beyond our personal sense of identity. Every system of transpersonal psychology states that enlightenment requires of us a cooperative relationship with influences bigger than ourselves. It is this feature of will which counterbalances the preceding one which emphasizes self-determination and personal choice. This is the paradox of power. The will empowers us to choose freely and determine our own life direction. But simultaneously the will offers us another option: to be empowered by something Greater through an obedient willingness. The will allows forces and influences from beyond the personal sphere to motivate and shape our lives. Although the word "obedience" is not a popular one, it is an essential requirement for the spiritual journey.

Changer. The will allows us to reshape our lives, even though we already have strong habits and tendencies. For every individual there is a certain momentum to life which, if allowed to play itself out, would result in very predictable outcomes. However, through the will we can change those patterns. An idea from Edgar Cayce's philosophy of the will is relevant here. It suggests that 20% of the influence in our lives can be measured by exterior signs or indicators (from psychological profiles to astrology or numerology), but the remaining 80% is under the influence of will. In other words, every condition based upon our past can be altered by the will.

However, when we can claim this potential for change, we must combine it with a sense of patience. The capacity to change patterns does not always mean that the change can be accomplished immediately. Much of the misunderstanding and misrepresentation of the will has been a distortion of this particular attribute. Yes, we *can* change things in our lives but, if we attempt it with impatience, then it frequently leads to unhappy conclusions.

Opposer of Mind. The most intriguing feature of the will is that it stands in opposition to mind. The significance of this principle should not be underestimated. Our tendency may be to dismiss this idea in a cursory fashion, noting its obvious truth from daily life experiences. Admittedly, there are ways in which we frequently experience how the will opposes a tendency of the mind. For example, the mind tells us that it wants an extra piece of dessert and the will may play a role to oppose or oppress that desire pattern. Or the mind wants to play and replay thoughts of self-pity, but the will may intervene to oppose this tendency by giving attention to a more cheerful outlook. However, the essential opposition between mind and will is something even more profound than these familiar situations from daily living might suggest. In Chapter 4 of this book we will develop a model for the ways in which mind and will interact, a model which illustrates a theory of the soul's evolution and which is based on this notion of opposition.

Developer. The will stands at the heart of the soul's spiritual development. Through the way in which the will is applied, the result is either evolution or "de-evolution"—either soul development or soul retrogression. Why is the will so central to soul development? It is because the goal of soul development is: to fully know our own individuality, yet simultaneously to be one with the whole of life. The will individualizes us and allows us to have this self-reflective knowledge of ourselves. So its proper use is an essential requirement of spiritual evolution. In addition, the will can foster oneness. As the personal will is brought into harmony with the divine will, the experience of oneness with God is made possible.

Motivator. The will gets us moving in life. Mind can provide for us a pattern of thinking, feeling or acting; but unless there is an impetus initiated by the will toward action, there are never results. A person in whom the will is slumbering is a person of little motivation, a person who is indifferent. Yet as that same person learns to awaken and train the will, the possibilities for action and change come alive.

Guide. The will can guide the mind. If "mind is the builder" we might well ask, "But what is it that directs or guides that building process?" In other words, if the functionings of mind can be symbolized by a builder or carpenter, we should wonder what it is that serves as the foreman or even the architect of this building job. If the will is asleep, then this building proceeds in a haphazard fashion, and each carpenter on the job may be building what he thinks the finished product ought to look like, only to discover that the results are unusable. However, as a kind of hidden soul power, we have the potential within us to shape our lives. The will can guide and direct the creative workings of the mind.

In summary, we have nine key ingredients which begin to formulate a new understanding of the human will. As we expand our picture of the will and how it operates in our lives, we can build on these fundamental characteristics:

> active principle
> individualizer
> chooser
> agent of obedience
> changer
> opposer of mind
> developer
> motivator
> guide

The Slumbering Seed of Your Future

Let's return to the most intriguing feature in this new understanding of will—its opposition to mind. Our life experience is a byproduct of the creative tension between these two elements of the soul. Life is an interplay of mental images and will.

Mental images are principally associated with our past. This makes sense if we think back to the concept that mind is the builder. In other words, the mind is an active force within us that can give a pattern or shape to the life force which we call spirit. When the mind works with pure creative energy to give it a pattern, that mental image continues to have existence long after its creation. We've all heard the phrase "thoughts are things." It simply means that once the mind has built something through its attitudes or emotions, what it has created continues over time. The products of the mind live on.

We might go so far as to make this claim, which at first may sound ridiculous:

Anything which appears as an image or a form really belongs to the *past*.

What *are* the images and forms referred to in this statement? Your dream images. The form of your physical body. Mental images that pop into your mind from familiar attitudes and emotions. Anything that you can see in the material world. All of these things are images and forms. As incredible as it may sound, they are all a reflection of something built by someone's mind *in the past*.

In contrast to the past orientation of mental images, the will is like a seed—it is of your future. The will draws you toward that which you are to become. The will is the principal agent of spiritual evolution.

But which is more real—mental images or will? Which of the two gives you the best sense of who you really are? Clearly the answer is will.

The greatest mistake we can make is to identify our sense of personal identity with mental images. We hinder our own spiritual development when we identify ourselves with the past instead of with the seed of what we are evolving toward.

The will has a kind of evolutionary wisdom. It is not the kind of repressive will that we would use to keep from eating an extra dessert, but a deeper will that is usually sleeping within us—a will toward enlightenment. This sleeping, unconscious will provides an impetus from deep within us toward wholeness.

But what about the other, more familiar side of the coin— the conscious will? We cannot ignore the significance of conscious will and its proper use. But it can be understood, trained, and properly developed only if we see a bigger picture. The conscious will must come to reflect the deeper, wiser will.

But if it is unconscious, how can we hope to experience it? One way is through true *imagination*. Imagination can reveal to us the direction toward our future, the way the will attempts to lead us. Something within us resonates strongly to or is sympathetic with this seed of our future. Out of this kind of soul level sympathy can arise truly imaginative insight and experience. Here imagination does not mean a re-experiencing of memories from our past. It's not saying to ourselves, "I imagined I was back in my third grade classroom." Instead it is imagination which is visionary, often having an element of surprise or wonder to it. It is will-directed imagination which leads us to a future which is fresh and new.

In addition to imagination, there is a second way in which we can experience the workings of this deepest will of the soul. It involves a great sensitivity to the *feeling* level of human experience. Here we must see that there are three levels of activity within us. The first is "thinking," a function which is relatively awake and immediately accessible for us. The second function is "feeling," which for us is not so much awake but instead analogous to dream-like experiences; that is to say, feeling is a way by which we can know things but which hasn't fully awakened within us, and is usually dimly perceived—just as our dreaming experiences are usually not as direct and conscious as our waking ones.

The third function is, of course, "willing." Our experience of the genuine will of the soul, or our lack of experience of it, is analogous to sleep. To repeat: We are fully awake as *thinking* beings, we only perceive or know in a hazy dreamlike fashion through our *feeling* function, and we are asleep in relationship to the real *willing* of the soul.

However, because feeling occupies a role *between* thinking and willing, it provides an indirect way in which we can experience the real will of the soul. Often by paying careful attention to the feelings which arise within us, we can learn the nature of this deeper sleeping faculty. Through nurturing the feeling side of ourselves, we can discover something about the nature of this seed within us, this great impetus toward our soul's destiny. We should keep in mind, however, that the term "feeling" describes something more subtle than emotions. Often our emotions are mental images which draw our attention to the past—even urging us to repeat the past. In contrast to this, an experience of our *feelings* gives us a way of *knowing* (usually a "knowing without knowing how").

What does our feeling nature perceive? If it is not emotions (which belong more to the mental images we have built in the past), then what is it? Perhaps this "knowing through feeling" comes from a sensitivity to the deep, unconscious will of the soul. Will allows us to feel finer influences reaching us from a higher level. In contrast, our lives are usually directed and shaped by influences arising from the physical world of cause and effect. Our tendency is to be buffeted about by life, merely reacting to outside, material forces. In this familiar state, the will is not operative and we are asleep—spiritually "asleep." Although we walk around through life with our eyes open, a more realistic analysis of our human condition is that we are asleep to our real nature. We don't feel influences coming to us from a higher realm.

Personality and Individuality

For most of our lives we operate from a level which we could call "personality." This important concept will be developed in depth in Chapter 4. However, for a moment let's consider the basic features of the personality, because it relates to the difference between what is usually called "will" and the "Real Will" of the soul.

The personality is a collection of habitual ways of thinking and feeling and acting. To a large extent it has been learned—taken on through imitation from those around us. This learning certainly begins in earliest childhood but continues through our adult years. The personality is not our real self. There is instead something deeper within us, what we might call "individuality" or the "Real I." It is our true identity as a spiritual being.

The personality itself is not a single identity and herein lies a great problem for us. The personality is made up of a collection of separate "I's" or subpersonalities. Each "I" is a distinct identity or role into which we fall from time to time in familiar life conditions.

For example, Janet is a 45-year-old businesswoman and mother of three children, ages 20, 14 and 9. In the course of a typical day her sense of personal identity shifts many times. She acts out many different roles as conditions around her change. By carefully observing her, we would come to see these distinct "I's" within her, and we might label each one or give each a number. Janet #1 is the subpersonality she identifies with whenever she and her husband are getting along well—"the content wife." Janet #2 is the tense, anxious "I" who interacts with her 20-year-old son—quite different than Janet #3 who has a relaxed relationship with her 9-year-old daughter.

At the office there are many different Janet subpersonalities: "the supportive boss," "the frazzled executive," and "the optimistic planner." In fact, dozens of different personality "I's" make up this collection which friends, family, and co-workers call "Janet." But at the level of personality, she is not a single identity.

For Janet, and for each of us, an ever-repeating shift from one "I" to another keeps us from a consistent sense of who we are. As forces and influences from material life nudge or push us toward identifying with a particular subpersonality "I," we forget the existence of other "I's." In actuality we live our lives with a multitude of "I's"; however, we like to pretend that we have a consistent identity.

Each subpersonality "I" has associated with it a set of habit patterns. These mechanical, automatic ways of thinking, feeling, and acting create a certain character for each subpersonality. Each subpersonality has its own agenda of desires and intentions, and in this fashion we might say that each has a will of its own. In other words, what is comonly called "will" is in truth just one of these personality wills or at best a compromise among the diverse wills of many different subpersonality "I's." However, this is not the authentic, deeper will of the soul. This is not what we can label "Real Will."

Real Will is that which sensitizes us to influences which arise from outside of material laws of cause and effect.

What are these higher influences? They are the forces of life which help us to synthesize, to be creative, and to provide meaningful solutions to life's problems. Real Will allows us to recognize new possibilities in situations where we have seen only a dilemma. It has a quality of patience and receptivity to it, since it requires us to be receptive to these influences which come from a higher level.

As the spiritual teacher, P.D. Ouspensky, once said: "Real Will is like suddenly seeing the solution to a mathematical problem." Haven't we all had that experience in life, where a new possibility or solution is suddenly presented to our minds? It usually comes after a period of intense work with the intellectual mind and effort with the conscious will. Yet the eventual solution comes to us as a *gift*, as we are open and receptive to its direction. This notion of Real Will is quite different from the traditional view of will which negates, suppresses, or attempts to force an issue. Maurice Nicoll wrote these words about the will as presented by his two teachers, P.D. Ouspensky and G.I. Gurdjieff:

> Mr. O. [i.e., Ouspensky] refers to a different idea of will. It is something that finds right solutions. It unites separate things, it arranges in right order, and so creates something new. It contains the idea of new *possibilities* . . . It has to do with a certainty that a solution is *possible*, and with a certain kind of active patience towards the at-present unsolved situation, where one does not as yet see the next connection . . . G. [i.e., Gurdjieff] once said that "patience is the Mother of Will." There *is* some solution. There *is* some possibility . . . Out of every situation it is possible to get meaning. Things apparently diverse can be brought into some unity of meaning. It is like asking and waiting. (*Psychological Commentaries*, p. 482)

A Parable of the Will

Sometimes a story or parable is helpful in understanding a complex subject. One of the best examples of a teaching parable about the will comes from G.I. Gurdjieff, a

Russian-born teacher of spiritual development who worked in the first half of this century. This parable is the story of the Horse, Carriage, and Driver.

In this allegory, which depicts the inner human state, we are shown how three levels—body, emotion, and intellect —are not in right relationship to one another. The parable begins by supposing that the driver of a horse and carriage has abandoned and forgotten his duties. He is drunk in a public bar, wasting his money, and in his drunkenness he thinks that his status is that of a master instead of a servant. The horse is unfed and weakening, and its reins are in disarray or lost. The carriage has fallen into poor condition. The master is away from the scene and will not return to ride in the carriage until the driver is back on the box of the carriage and everything is in order.

In this parable the carriage represents the human body, the horse represents the emotions, and the driver the intellectual mind. The state of drunkenness depicts the typical condition of our human minds. It stands for a kind of imagining which is based upon the past, the constant flow of mental images from our past with which we so readily identify. In our own "drunkenness" we mechanically shift from one subpersonality to the next, reacting to influences from material life. We are under the illusion that we are masters of ourselves and of our destiny, when in fact these three essential levels of our being are not at all in harmonious relationship to one another. Body, emotion, and intellect are not synchronized.

According to this parable, what must happen? First, the driver must awaken to understand his state. He must stop his drunken imaginings and momentarily disidentify from his familiar state of mind long enough to recognize the condition into which he has fallen. Then, he must leave the public drinking house and go out and repair the carriage (i.e., care for his physical body), and attend to the needs of the horse (i.e., the emotional self). Once this is done the driver can lift himself up onto the box. Then, he can regain the reins and hold them firmly in hand. It is only at this point that the master can return to the scene and occupy his position within the carriage; it is only when the driver has

done everything he can to set things in proper order that the
master can come back. However, in this parable the master
does not immediately give directions for proceeding. The
driver must begin the movement of horse and carriage in the
direction that he thinks best and then listen intently for
corrective guidance from the master within the carriage.

This is a parable of extraordinary depth and insight for
us, and it illustrates a number of places in which the human
will plays a critical role. The will is an indispensable agent
in that awakening which initiates a change in conditions. It
is the will which directs attention and allows certain
thoughts and emotions to shape our sense of identity. It is,
therefore, through an active will that we are able to
disidentify from old familiar personality states and
awaken enough to recognize from a spiritual point of view
the hopeless condition into which we have placed
ourselves. This is accomplished through the systematic
practice of an exercise Gurdjieff called self-observation. It
is a matter of gaining a kind of inner separation so that one
"stands aside and watches self go by." Through an active
will we are able to create an observing identity which
objectively and noncritically is able to separate from the
strong habit patterns which have kept us in a "drunken
state."

This work of self-observation shall, we hope, lead us to a
new respect for our physical and emotional bodies. We may
find it possible to start changing many of the ways in which
we treat ourselves physically and emotionally and begin to
achieve new health at these levels. But the actual goal of
self-observation is something even more specific: to
remember the real self. Through this exercise of will, we
can stand aside and observe the habit patterns of
personality. We can finally reach a state in which we
remember the real self—that essential identity called
individuality. It is at this point that the will leads us to a
dramatic shift in consciousness, symbolized in the parable
by the driver climbing up to a new level and sitting on the
box of the carriage.

But even when moments of this self-remembering are
achieved, there remains a problem. The driver does not yet

have the reins in hand. The reins symbolize a connection or link between the emotions and thought. Haven't we all frequently experienced the lack of these reins? Our emotions rarely seem to follow in the direction that our thoughts would like, so some connecting discipline is needed. Once again we find, then, an important role for the will to play. A linkage between the horse and driver can be created by the use of purposeful, directed imagination and visualization. The language of the horse is not the same as that of the driver. The mind operates by reasoned thought but the emotions speak a language of imagery. Nicoll puts it this way:

> The horse understands visual language, the driver words, and the parable connects the two. Visual imagery is a universal language. It is the language of signs. The horse only understands a universal language of visual images. That is why, if you wish to control the horse from the mind, you must visualize and not merely think. One of the things that we are taught in this Work is visualization. You must visualize what you have thought of in regard to your behavior . . . (*Psychological Commentaries*, p. 467)

The role of the will in helping to create these reins is twofold. On the one hand, we can use the conscious will to purposely direct the mind toward specific visualization. But on the other hand, we might expect a deeper will, what we have called the Real Will, to influence us in a similar way through the imagination. This is a kind of *inspired imagination.* In other words, *Real Will can operate on the imaginative forces of the mind to create the very images which can harmonize the activities of thought and emotion.*

The parable illustrates another role of the human will in regard to the problem of obtaining guidance. We should take careful note that in this allegory the driver is required to first start the horse and carriage moving, based upon his own best understanding. This shows us something about how to work with inner guidance. We should expect that oftentimes Real Will shall make its intentions evident to us only after we have used the conscious will to set things in motion, only after we have initiated a direction which we tentatively feel is right.

At this point, we come to the conclusion of the parable and its final teaching to us about the will. Once the carriage is set in motion, the driver must be attentive. The hallmark of the will is attentiveness. We can develop a relationship with Real Will only to the extent that we are able to be receptive and responsive. Once again we confront the paradoxical truth: The will is experienced in our lives in an *active* as well as a *receptive* mode.

Summary of a New Understanding

We have covered a considerable amount of ground thus far in developing new definitions of the nature of the will. Perhaps the most important principle is that the will should be appreciated for its extraordinary potential to influence, shape, and direct spiritual growth. But let's keep in mind six other key concepts, which shall be developed further in later chapters as we examine the qualities of the will, the stages of its development, and the ways in which the will can influence us in daily living.

1. Will is a fundamental building block. We have compared it to one of the primary pigment colors. Along with energy and mind, the will is a fundamental ingredient which determines our experience.

2. The will has both a conscious and an unconscious component. It was an extraordinary discovery for humanity when the unconscious nature of the human mind was recognized, and it is an equally significant discovery to find that there is an unconscious level at which the will operates. In fact, a deeper will, more consistent with our real spiritual nature, exists and subtly influences us in waking life if we are attentive to it.

3. The will is our future. In this case we are speaking largely of the unconscious component of the will which is sensitive to our spiritual destiny and continually provides us with influences in daily life serving to draw us toward that future. We might even say that this Real Will, coming from our future, can influence the present, particularly through the experience of inspired imagination and feeling.

4. The will stands in contrast to the mind. Just as influences from Real Will relate to our future, the mind most often operates from the level of the past. It is the nature of the mind to repeat familiar memory patterns. Even its capability to analyze logically is usually directed toward forms and content which are more related to the past than they are to the future.

Yet, despite this fundamental opposition between mind and will, there is the possibility for cooperation and harmony. We shall see later that cooperation is possible only if the mind plays an obedient role to the will—only if the mind serves the sense of purpose and direction offered by the will can this cooperative relationship be formed. As long as the mind, with its orientation toward the past, insists upon playing the superior role, the will is left largely in a "sleeping" state.

5. The will is that which gives us our individuality. It is not our thoughts which give us our individuality, but instead it is the capacity to know that we have thoughts. The ability to be self-reflective and stand outside ourselves makes us unique individuals. We experience our specialness in creation because of the capability which the will gives us to be self-reflective. Using the will we can stand aside from or disidentify from our thoughts enough to recognize that we even have them.

By way of analogy, consider what happens in a lucid dream (a dream in which you know that you are in fact in the dream state). In a lucid dream the will has awakened. In a lucid dream you know of your own individuality as a dreamer, not because you are having thought-form dream images before your awareness, but instead because you are momentarily able to step aside and become self-reflective, recognizing that it is a dream going on about you.

The same principles hold true in waking life. We can learn to go through daily living in a lucid fashion, and it is the will which allows us to have this self-reflective consciousness which knows its own individuality. This is a subtle, and perhaps to some people insignificant, distinction; and yet if we recognize and work with this insight about the significance of the will, it opens up to us a whole array of approaches and techniques for personal and spiritual growth. If we can recognize that our very identity as a unique creation rests upon the divine birthright of the free will, then we begin to see its importance and its power in shaping our destiny.

6. We know the will's reality most directly through attention. Despite all of these references to an unconscious Real Will, it is crucial for us to work with awakening and training the will as it is experienced at a *conscious* level. The most immediate way in which we are able to do this is through the capacity to direct attention. The exercise of directing attention can be applied to the outer world of sensory perceptions as well as to our inner world of thought and emotion.

RECOMMENDED ADDITIONAL READING

The Edgar Cayce Primer, Herbert Puryear (Bantam Books, New York, 1982)

The highlights of the system of thought found in Cayce's readings are presented in a highly readable format. A good introduction for those who want an overview of the psychological, philosophical, and theological perspective in this psychically derived material.

The Gurdjieff Work, Kathleen Speeth (Harper and Row, New York, 1976)

This is perhaps the best summary of Gurdjieff's system and is written by a woman with a tremendous gift for explaining and clarifying complex subjects. A psychotherapist by profession, Speeth knew Gurdjieff personally, having spent some of her early years with her parents at Gurdjieff's Institute outside Paris.

In Search of the Miraculous, P.D. Ouspensky (Harcourt, Brace and Javanovich, New York, 1949)

An autobiographical account of Ouspensky's years with Gurdjieff, this book is perhaps the most readable of all Ouspensky's works. It also gives an excellent survey of key principles from Gurdjieff's system as seen through the eyes of who many people feel is his most brilliant student.

"Rudolf Steiner: Initiate of the Will" in *Work Arising,* John Davy, editor (Rudolf Steiner Press, London, 1975)

An excellent biographical essay which features the importance Steiner placed on the soul faculty of willing. This essay is the introduction to the anthology which Davy edited. The collection documents modern initiatives to apply Steiner's ideas in social, medical, artistic, religious, and educative disciplines.

"Individual Spiritual Development and Human Freedom" in *Man and World in the Light of Anthroposophy,* Stewart Easton (Anthroposophic Press, Spring Valley, N.Y., 1975)

This lengthy work is arguably the best summary of Steiner's ideas. Easton is a longtime scholar of these teachings and does a masterful job in making them more understandable. The chapter cited above—Chapter 3—deals specifically with the nature of thinking and willing as described by Steiner in *The Philosophy of Freedom*.

Study of Man, Rudolf Steiner (Rudolf Steiner Press, London, 1966)

This series of lectures was given to the faculty of the original Waldorf School in Germany in 1919. There is considerable material about educating the will. This is not an easy book to read. But those who have familiarized themselves with Steiner's basic ideas (such as can be found by reading the Stewart Easton volume), shall find very important concepts about the will in lectures 4, 5, and 6.

CHAPTER THREE

Qualities of the Will

In order to understand fully the importance of the human will, we must extend our exploration further. As we have seen in the previous two chapters, a strong case can be made for the reality and significance of the will. It is a characteristic of our being distinct from mind and energy, a central feature in our quest for spiritual enlightenment.

But each of us is left to wonder, "How exactly do I experience my will? By what qualities can my will be recognized?" This kind of question does not ask about the development of the will, a topic to be addressed in a later chapter. Instead it addresses the very way by which we experience the reality of the will in our daily lives.

This chapter examines seven qualities of the human will. Some of these features may sound like states of *mind*. Recognizing this, we may be tempted to slip back into thinking of the will as a special aspect of the mind. But this problem can be avoided by realizing that we know of the will's existence by the states of mind or sensations of body which it *produces* in life experiences. In other words, *the will often has a transparent nature*, it often seems invisible and reveals itself by the physical and mental characteristics which it stimulates.

We observe the same phenomenon with the wind. We don't observe the wind itself but, instead, its effects, as leaves rustle on treetops and discarded papers blow across our path. A similar condition exists with the nature of light. Light itself does not take on physical form and yet it illuminates physical forms so that we can see them. In the same way, the will does not take a physical form and yet we can experience its qualities by the effects it has upon physical conditions. It is not an energy and yet we can understand its nature by the way it directs energy. The will is not a state of mind, but we feel its existence by the attitudes and emotions it awakens.

The analogy of light can be extended further if we recall that white light can be broken down into seven spectral colors. Likewise, the human will has within it distinct characteristics. Different life situations provide the opportunity for the will to express itself in various characteristic ways. This chapter explores seven qualities of the will, each of which is in some stage of awakening within you. You may recognize that some of these characteristics are ones to which you already have easy access—they are strengths within your character. Others you may recognize as major areas of weakness. Just as pure light is created by the balanced integration of all the colors of the spectrum, each of these qualities of will is necessary for a full awakening of the will's potential within you.

These seven qualities were first proposed by Roberto Assagioli, an Italian physician who lived in the first half of this century. At his death in 1974 Assagioli left a remarkable legacy of psychological insights and techniques. His system is called "psychosynthesis" and it is described in great detail in his two principal books, *Psychosynthesis* and *The Act of Will.* Assagioli's system is one of the finest psychologies with a spiritual orientation ever developed. One of the features that makes psychosynthesis such an extraordinary system is the detail in which Assagioli has documented the role of the will in psychological health. Although only one portion of his book *The Act of Will* deals with the seven qualities of will, it is the section which many readers find most straightforward and immediately applicable.

The sequence in which this chapter presents the seven qualities of will is not the order in which Assagioli introduces them. Here they are arranged in a specific sequence, for a purpose which shall be evident at the conclusion of the chapter.

Each of the qualities of the will can be examined in terms of the way we experience it when the will is *healthy.* But, in contrast to this, we can note what it is that we experience when this particular quality of will is unawakened. In addition, we can recognize that each of these seven qualities of will has a caricature or impostor (such as "stubbornness" posing for "patient persistence"). These bogus qualities resemble the genuine qualities of will; and yet, upon careful scrutiny, they are exposed as lacking the real nature of the human will. It is particularly critical to our understanding of the will that we be able to distinguish between the real qualities and their caricature. The will has long been distorted and misrepresented largely because we have been unable to make this distinction. These caricature qualities of will psychologically play a role that can be called the "surrogate will." They operate in the individual's life in a way that so closely resembles the nature of true will that a person may mistakenly assume that the will is healthy. In fact, the will is asleep, and a replacement state of mind has usurped its rightful position.*

The caricature qualities of will have their origin in a fear or a guilt which is often unconscious, yet powerfully influential. They serve not to initiate change and growth for the individual, but to perpetuate the status quo. No careful study of the seven qualities of will would be complete without an examination of how this illusory, surrogate will imitates certain features of real will, yet lacks its essential ingredients. Those essential ingredients of Real Will are as follows:

1. A Dynamic, Energetic Way of Relating to Life

There is an energy fount in the universe, and, as a spiritual creation with free will, you have access to that resource. Yes, there is a physical, mechanistic law of the universe called "entropy," which suggests that the universe is running down. If life is observed as purely physical processes, this law of entropy accurately predicts and describes conditions in the material world. But now

---

*The author credits the concept of surrogate will to David Aberegg, a researcher and lecturer at the Association for Research and Enlightenment, Inc., in Virginia Beach, Virginia.

from theological and philosophical as well as scientific circles comes speculation that there is a complementary law—a law of syntropy. Conscious, living things of the universe may be special points into which an unlimited energy resource can flow. As a being of free will, you have the capability to create a direct relationship with that limitless supply of energy. This is the first and most fundamental quality of your will.

Your will creates for you an energetic relationship with life by freeing you from energy-sapping patterns of your mind. Those patterns are attitudinal and emotional tendencies which leach your energy, leaving you frustrated and in despair. An act of your will—an act of will drawing upon this first quality—allows you to separate (to "disidentify") from those energy-sapping mental patterns.

Consider, for example, Rebecca, who is a mother and part-time substitute high school teacher. Rebecca is a worrier. She worries about whether or not her children will do well enough in high school to gain admission to a prestigious university; she worries about her husband's career; and, she worries about her own health, allowing the slightest physical discomfort to stimulate imaginings of impending serious illnesses. Over the years Rebecca has built and rebuilt a complex set of attitudes and emotions all related to this habitual tendency for worrying. As she gives attention to this pattern of mind, as she allows herself to be so identified with it, it saps and drains her spiritual life force. The quality of her will which might make things different is asleep. So, more and more fully, Rebecca's life is governed by the law of entropy. By relating to herself and to life primarily through its physical, material dimension and by allowing this first quality of will to remain dormant, she finds that she is often weak, overwhelmed, and unable to do anything but let her life drift on with its own momentum.

What would happen if Rebecca could experience the awakening of this first quality of will? It would allow her to say "no" to these habitual patterns of mind which have made her the worrier. Her will could give her empowerment in life. She would experience not only a new access to creative life force, but she would also become a *dynamic* person.

The will is dynamic because it gives you the possibility to make changes in your life. When the will is asleep, your life is static. When the will is unawakened, you merely drift along through life allowing habitual patterns of mind to shape your sense of self-identity and your responses to challenges. However, this first quality of will can move you from a static condition to a dynamic one. The will allows Rebecca to end the hold which these worrying patterns of mind have exerted on her. It allows her to discover that she is empowered to act creatively about each of the areas of life over which she has always worried.

For Rebecca or for you, this first quality of will may manifest as a kind of "quiet enthusiasm" for life. Having a dynamic, energetic way of relating to life does not necessarily mean a boisterous, extroverted enthusiasm. Because each of us has a different temperament, these qualities of will can manifest in somewhat different ways. The key, however, to this first quality of will is the way in which it gives us a greater access to a universal fount of spiritual energy, allowing and empowering us to make creative changes in life.

We must take great care, however, that we not confuse this genuine quality of will with an imposter: a manic or "hyper" kind of behavior that often looks like dynamism but originates in deep psychological imbalances. The manic personality invariably shifts to depression in a short period of time. In its most extreme condition, it reverts to the psychotic state of a manic-depressive individual.

In a related fashion, the "hyper" person is usually someone who is quickly draining herself through busy behavior that looks energetic. This caricature of the first quality of will does not build for her a relationship with the infinite resource of the universe. Instead it draws out and quickly burns up personal energies. It is rarely if ever able to make the kind of genuine life changes which characterize a dynamic existence.

2. Discipline and Control

It should surprise no one that the ability to discipline and control our lives is a feature of the will. In fact, for some people this is the sole quality to which they can easily relate. Unfortunately the stereotyped notions of both self-discipline and self-control fail to do justice to this feature of the will. A broader and healthier view of the role of discipline in personal growth is needed.

What is also required is an understanding of self-control that truly integrates the human personality, instead of dividing it.

Three factors can help you keep this second quality of the will both awake *and* functioning in a way that aids your growth. First, there is a need for self-control to be linked to *vision* or a sense of *personal ideal*. Will operates best in relationship to the present and the future. When you have a vision of how you want your attitudes and behaviors of today to help shape your future, then self-control can more easily stay healthy.

The second key factor is *affirmation* as opposed to negation. When you try to use your will's capacity for self-discipline, which of these two options happens most often?

> Things I am going to *do*
> Things I am *not* going to *do*

Does your personal voice of the disciplining will say things like "Don't eat desserts" or "Don't be late" or "Don't skip exercising"? Certainly there is a place for using the will to refrain from doing things. However, there is a strong tendency in most all of us to view discipline exclusively in this negative way.

Just as easily, discipline can be affirming. You can use your will to "do." For example, the voice of the disciplining will can also say "Do take time daily to meditate" or "Do spend some time just playing with your kids" or "Do read a new book every two weeks."

Finally, the factor of *creativity* helps to keep the disciplining, controlling will healthy. Remember that will is the faculty of your soul which stands in opposition to your mind, especially the habits which your mind so potently holds. Sometimes your most disciplined acts can become static, rigid, "positive" habits which have lost all sensitivity to the real needs of the moment. Subtly, something that started out as an expression of real will can turn into unconscious ruts of the mind. This principle is illustrated at one point in the story of Eric, whose will is in disarray at the level of this second quality: discipline and control.

Eric is an energetic, affable 30-year-old carpenter and painter. He is frustrated in his vocational life because it seems like a dead end: he has been unable to reach a supervisory position with any company for which he has worked. Yet the obstacle to his promotion is obvious. He lacks the ability to discipline himself and to gain control over his life. Both at home and on the job, he lacks a sense of direction. His philosophy of life is that whatever is going to happen will happen. Eric has an admirable aptitude for letting things flow and unfold in their own way, but it is not balanced by any capacity to organize himself in relation to a clear ideal for his future. He has no ability to be co-creative with God, because he lacks the skill to control his thinking, feeling, and acting along the pathway of a personal ideal. The second quality of his will is asleep.

Sadly, he even fails to exhibit a healthy disciplining will in the one area of his life where he thinks he has achieved it. Four times a week he shows up at a local exercise gymnasium and completes a 45-minute weight-lifting routine. The only interruption to this pattern occurs when he has injured himself in one of the weight-lifting machines. But these mishaps occur with great regularity. Invariably they happen because Eric is determined to force his body to accomplish the 45-minute routine no matter what the extenuating circumstances may be. If he is sick or low on energy one day, he will still "discipline" himself to complete all his regular weight exercises, and often he will strain a muscle in so doing.

What started out as a genuine act of a healthy disciplining will has now subtly become something else. He is trapped and enslaved by his own discipline. What began as a promising effort to demonstrate self-control has now become something that controls him.

What is now missing for Eric is a will which is creative in

its disciplining, controlling function. What Eric needs is to awaken a will that is sensitive to the conditions of each day rather than stuck in rigid habits that literally hurt him physically. What he needs, as well, is a disciplining, controlling will that can help him affirm his talents in order to achieve his potential. When this second quality of his will awakens, Eric can get himself organized to be co-creative in shaping a positive, hopeful future.

However, what Eric *doesn't* need is a caricature of this quality of will: repression. Here is the familiar image of "willpower," this imposter quality which usurps the place of a healthy disciplining will. Repression may look like self-control and it may promise growth, but it is really a function of mind acting as surrogate will. Usually motivated by a fear (that may be conscious or unconscious), repression divides the human personality and attempts to "keep the lid on" by denial. Despite its temporary success at achieving self-control, it always fails in the end because that which is repressed doesn't go away.

Instead, a healthy will, manifesting through the quality of self-discipline, says to desires, drives, and appetites, "Your value is appreciated; your energy will be given an appropriate outlet and timing." In sharp contrast, the caricature quality of repression says to those same things within you, "Go away! You are unacceptable in any form and at any time. Let's pretend you don't exist." Psychoanalysts have graphically demonstrated the failure of "willpower" to integrate successfully the personality when it acts through repression. In Jungian terms, the repressed features of yourself merely become a part of your own shadow personality (a topic to be explored more fully in a later chapter on the powers of good and evil).

3. Courageous Initiative

Initiative means "the ability to get new things started." Your will is the key to creating new directions for your life. This quality of will initiates novel patterns of living which move you out of the ruts and static habits of your past.

Of course, the creation of new ways of thinking, feeling, and acting involves the mind as well. "Mind is the builder," but it can function in an initiating way only when the will acts to free the mind from its habit patterns. "Will is the director," spurring the mind to the creation of new patterns for living.

The kind of initiative suggested by this third quality of will can relate to both inner and outer changes. Sometimes it means starting different ways of acting in the world. The shy person might begin to speak up more often as an act of will; or, the talkative individual might start to listen more.

However, at a more fundamental level the initiating will works for an *inner* change. Through it you create a new perspective of yourself and shape a new sense of personal identity. Although the natural tendency is to think of your power to initiate as an outwardly active one, it must be coupled to the more basic inner initiative of new identity.

The word "courageous" is another appropriate description of how you experience this quality of your will. To start something new requires a brave willingness to let go of the old—usually before the new is fully at hand. If you honestly evaluate yourself, you can probably observe the strong tendency to hang on tightly to the familiar ways *until* the newly created ways are complete. However, personal change usually won't work that way. You must live like a circus trapeze artist who lets go of one swing and dangles in space for a moment before grasping the next swing. Only with courage is that possible. Human growth is achieved only when you have faith in what you are initiating and creating, and thereby courageously let go of the familiar ways of acting or of seeing yourself.

To illustrate this quality, consider the case of Emily, a 62-year-old grandmother and wife of a retired businessman. Emily feels victimized, but not because things are overtly wrong with her life. Her health is reasonably good, she has a family who cares for her, and her material needs are more than adequately met. Yet, because this quality of her will is asleep, she feels boxed in.

All the significant people in her life share a common image of Emily, and she is restless because she feels that she is a victim of their expectations. She never does anything new or unusual since she is so busy conforming to the way everybody assumes she will be. Lacking access to her courageous initiating will, Emily timidly settles for the way things have always been. In relationship to her husband, she gives in to their habitual roles in which he makes all the family financial decisions and she makes all the family social decisions. In relationship to her son, she continues to play a familiar role of nagging and prodding him to take more time for relaxation. In her community, Emily always plays the part of the "second-fiddle" helper in service clubs, doing all the behind-the-scenes work, yet never taking a leadership role.

However, it is within Emily's grasp to change her life, *if* she will claim the courageous, initiating quality of her will. It might start with an inner activity of her will which bravely surrenders the old way of seeing herself. It can create the vision of a different way of feeling about her talents and how she wants to make use of them. Then, through courageous action she can begin to express this new way of knowing herself. Most likely she won't suddenly and radically alter the way she relates to the world around her. But in little ways she will begin to surprise people. She may speak her mind about an investment her husband plans to make, or ask him to play a bigger role in a family holiday celebration. Or she may startle everyone by offering herself for a leadership role at her church. The feeling of being boxed in and victimized can begin to dissipate, as this quality of her will awakens and gives her the power to be more creative.

What Emily doesn't need, though, is the caricature of this quality of will: reckless novelty. What poses as courage may be a hidden fear. This imposter is usually the result of fear-based efforts to bring outer change without making any inner changes at the same time. If Emily suddenly started doing new yet reckless things in her life, it wouldn't be a true act of will, although observers might mistakenly think that she had suddenly become a woman of great courage and strong will. This kind of surrogate willfulness is often recognized by its tendency for destructiveness. In contrast, courageous initiative builds new patterns and directions by adding on new dimenions rather than tearing down old ones.

4. Patient Persistence

The will allows us to live in ways which counter the *appearance* of things. By whatever word you choose to call it, there is a quality within you that can hold to an inner conviction, even when the outer perceptions or the inner memories of the mind suggest otherwise. You may experience it as persistence or commitment or dedication; but, however it happens in your life, it is an indispensable factor in growth.

As already noted many times before, it is the tendency of your mind to repeat the past. It takes persistence and commitment to change, because the mind can present countless reasons for you to abandon your dedication to positive change. But it is your will which gives you the power to "hang in there" and persistently work toward your ideals.

When this kind of dedication is coupled with real patience, then you have awakened to one of the most dramatic and little-understood qualities of the will. Patient persistence is difficult to grasp for people in our culture because it runs counter to the values and ethics of a technological, consumer society. Men and women of the industrialized Western world have "instantitis," a disease of the mind that expects all problems to be solved immediately. For example, people pop pills to remove pain instantaneously. They watch television dramas which subtly hypnotize them with the belief that most any dilemma can be resolved in one hour.

What is this mysterious factor of patience and how is it related to the will? The philosophy found in the Edgar Cayce readings refers to patience as an actual dimension of reality—a fundamental ingredient of how you can measure your experiences, just as time and space are dimensions. Patience measures how well you understand the purposes for what is happening in time and space. Patience is a way by which you can lift yourself out of the familiar reality which sees life as caught in time. In other words, patience doesn't necessarily mean waiting around for a long time. It doesn't mean suffering gladly for years and years. Patience is outside of time. Admittedly, once you have awakened the dimension of patience, you might find yourself choosing to wait for a long time or to suffer gladly for years and years with some problem. But it would be with a patience that brings you understanding.

The relationship between patience and will is intimate. Gurdjieff called patience "the mother of Real Will." As we become more patient, it lifts us to a new perspective of time and space. We see more clearly the purposes behind what is happening to us. We find it easier to be more persistent in working toward our ideals and goals.

When this quality of will is asleep, you may find yourself in a dilemma like the following example: George is a 50-year-old machinist foreman whose life is filled with disappointment. Throughout his adult life his *expectations* have almost never been met. What he expects of himself, and especially of other people, never measures up. The problem has now become even more serious because George and his family have recently moved to a new city. He has accepted a challenging new job, and he is full of more expectations.

But his disappointment has only been magnified in this new setting. The job hasn't turned out to be what he had hoped. The neighbors surrounding his new home are reasonably friendly, but there is not the strong bond of community he had wanted. George is even disappointed with himself. His new job requires some extra training and he is disappointed by his frequent failures to grasp many of the new skills he must learn.

What is the heart of George's problem? You might be tempted to say that he is just a hypercritical person. Certainly such a quality can easily lead to this kind of chronic disappointment for anyone. However, in this instance the problem stems from a failure of his will. George lacks the quality of will that would allow him to be patiently persistent in building self-esteem at his new job or in helping build stronger community bonds. When results don't come immediately and easily, George gives up very quickly out of impatience.

Of course, the solution for George does not lie with a caricature of will. In fact, there are two imposters that he must try to avoid as he strives to awaken his patiently persistent will. One form of the surrogate will is stubbornness. In this case, he could be persistent but lack the deeper understanding of his problems which comes by patience. People are often fooled by a stubborn individual, and they mistakenly assume that such a person must have a strong, healthy will. In fact, stubbornness is *at best* an activity only of an immature will, a will which is being distorted by fear.

The second caricature of will at this level is a kind of laid-back passivity that is easily mistaken for patience, but which lacks any persistent efforts to make changes. George could just "go with the flow," but that probably won't help his life. Again, people can be fooled by this behavior, assuming that only a healthy will could create such trust in life and be so patient. However, the understanding generated by true patience doesn't lead to passive inactivity. Instead, real patience produces persistent and dedicated commitments to active living.

5. Decisive, Resolute Choice

The most familiar quality of your will is the capacity to choose. It is the most direct way in which you experience the independent feature of your soul called will. Without your will, life would be predetermined and your existence would be reduced to a mechanical one.

But how free is your capacity to choose? Is everything that *feels* like a free will really so free? Behavioristic psychology insists that *any* feeling of free choice is illusory and that your selections in life are predetermined by your conditioning. The truth of the matter lies between two extremes.

The possibility of a middle ground is appropriate because there are many degrees of freedom. The question of will's freedom is not just between states of "fully on" or "fully off," like a light bulb on a standard switch. Rather there are many points along a continuum of freedom. The extent of your freedom to choose is like a light controlled by a dimmer switch. It can be set to many possible points between full illumination and complete darkness.

Probably much of what feels like free choice is actually very predictable and has a low degree of awakened will. For example, your selections from the menu last time you were in a restaurant may have felt like free-willed choices. But in fact they were probably highly conditioned ones that might have been predicted by anyone who knew your habits and taste preferences. Or, here is another but less obvious example: What about your quick decision to respond sarcastically to the criticism of a friend? It may have felt like a choice, but it really involved conditioned habit with little will.

On the other hand, you *do* have moments of genuine choice, times when a relatively free expression of your will is possible. Even though these moments may not happen as frequently as you would like to think they do (or as often as it is possible for them to occur!), there *are* opportunities to exercise your decisive, resolute will. If you are a meditator, it happens in those quiet moments as you focus attention. It happens whenever there are two equally attractive courses of action available to you—in your job or your family relations or in the way you treat yourself.

To understand the role that a healthy will plays in making resolute choices, consider this simple model of decision making. Although decisions you are forced to make often seem messier than this neat three-part scheme, it is still an instructive model to demonstrate how the will can function in either a healthy or a distorted way in confronting choices.

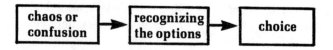

When your will is operating in an awakened and balanced fashion, you pass through all three of these stages for a time which is appropriate for the problem you face. Obviously there can be no set rules for the ideal amount of time to spend at each step. You don't have much time to move through all three stages when someone yells fire in a crowded restaurant and you smell smoke. On the other hand, if you have just gone through a divorce, it may be wise to spend plenty of time moving through these stages before deciding whether or not to marry again.

When the decision will is sleeping, you can get stuck at the first or second stage. The result is either a chronic sense of being mixed-up and confused, or it is a pattern of wishy-washy indecision that never gets beyond all the options. First, you need a healthy will just to be able skillfully to recognize the options. In other words, will is a factor not just at the moment of choice, but in a preliminary step that sees all the possibilities. One of the functions of real will is to see shades of meaning, to perceive finer and finer degrees of possibility in a situation. Only then does will play the more obvious role of decision making. You must have an awakened and balanced will to make effective choices from among the alternatives.

To illustrate this process, consider the case of Carol, a 38-year-old woman who has been divorced for four years. Her life is full of bitterness, not merely toward her ex-husband but also toward the people in her present life situation. She feels unappreciated and robbed of opportunities to be what she could have been. Despite a college degree in business, she has never been able to secure a meaningful position, but has instead bounced around from one part-time job to another. She has been unable to form any close relationship with a man since her divorce, not because of any avowed disinterest in doing so. Rather, her interpersonal relations suffer from the same problem as does her professional life: Carol has a sleeping will, especially in regard to its decisive, choosing quality.

She is a skillful person at recognizing alternatives but gets stuck at that step of the decision-making process. She sees dozens of promising career options in the local business world each year, but is never able to set her sights resolutely on one particular job and go after it. She has many male acquaintenances, a few of whom she knows would like to know her better. However, she is never able to make a choice and then invest the time and energy required to explore the relationship.

A number of psychological interpretations of Carol's

condition are obvious. Maybe she fears professional
success. Perhaps she is worried, for good reason, about
getting hurt again in marriage. But whatever perspective
one uses to analyze her situation, the conclusion remains
that her bitterness in life can be resolved only by
addressing her crisis with her personal will. Nothing can
get better until she begins to exercise her capacity to make
free choices.

As with the other qualities of will, there are caricatures
which must be avoided. An imposter will at this level is a
tendency to make decisions hurriedly, either skipping one
of the steps in the three-part process or just rushing the
timing. Each step is important, and effective choices can
rarely be made unless the first and second steps are
permitted to play their roles.

Confusion and chaos are signs of the old structures of life
breaking down so that something new can emerge. There is
nothing inherently unspiritual in feeling confused. In fact,
growth may not be possible without periods of chaos.
Disorientation is a way in which the strong habit patterns
of the personality are loosened so that a new pattern of the
deeper, more essential individuality can be born. It is a sign
of the person with a mature, healthy will that can stand the
discomfort of the confusion long enough to let genuinely
new, growth-oriented alternatives begin to emerge. To
rush the process usually leads to a set of alternatives,
which will re-create the old state of affairs. For example, if
Carol had a caricature of decisive will (rather than merely a
sleeping will), she might have tried to rush out of her
natural state of confusion after her divorce. Her imposter
will might immediately have tried to make the choice of a
new marriage partner, with a high likelihood of all
alternatives leading to another marriage like her first one.

Another form of the imposter will at this level is to make a
choice hurriedly, before all the necessary alternatives have
come into view. Of course, the problem one faces is how to
know when *enough* options are present. However, one
certainty is that seizing the *first* option which presents
itself is *not* the mark of a healthy will even though it may
fool many observers by its appearance of decisiveness.

Real Will requires at least two alternatives (and sometimes many more, depending on the problem) before it can exercise its quality of decisive, resolute choice.

6. One-Pointed, Focused Concentration

The capacity to concentrate and maintain a singleness of attention is reminiscent of a previous quality of the will: persistence. Whereas persistence is especially related to consistency in action, concentration is most closely tied to the inner, mental world. It is an act of will to identify a priority or ideal and then stay focused on it in a one-pointed way.

Although this quality of will is applicable to a wide assortment of life situations, it is especially required in the discipline of meditation. There are many schools of meditation and they give different instructions about *how* to use the one-pointed, focused will. However, almost all forms of this practice recognize the crucial role played by the will. In many meditation systems, the one-pointed, focused will is particularly important to the early stages of meditation. For example, in her classic study of Western contemplatives and mystics entitled *Mysticism*, Evelyn Underhill describes three progressive steps in "introversion" (i.e., meditation): recollection, the quiet, and contemplation.

Especially during the first stage, the will is needed for its capacity to concentrate and focus one-pointedly on the chosen ideal for meditation. This is the most difficult of three stages. It is what Underhill calls "a hard and ungrateful task," and it is well known to anyone who has tried to meditate. The mind does not easily surrender its habitual tendency to flit around from topic to topic, following any stimulus which offers the slightest novelty.

However, the role of one-pointed, focused will is not reserved merely for formalized efforts like meditation. Throughout the day you are challenged to awaken and make use of this quality. You are continually faced with opportunities to select priorities for how you may use your time, energy, and other resources. To what extent are you able to maintain a consistent attentiveness to the ideals and direction which you have chosen? Without this sixth quality of will, even the wisest decisions and choices you have made can produce little impact.

The key to the will's capacity to be one-pointed and focused is *attention*. As William James astutely pointed out nearly 100 years ago, the principal faculty of the will is its capacity to direct attention. When the will is asleep, your life is scattered and distracted. Attention bounces from one thing to the next. With no force to keep it in place or to give it direction, attention rests upon whatever is momentarily most stimulating.

But there is a specific strategy for strengthening this quality of the will. What is required in order to give the one-pointed will a *chance* to develop and mature? It must have a *focal point*, but not just any focal point. The developing will requires something very special to which it can direct attention. In order to have the best chance to awaken in a healthy, balanced way, it needs a focal point which relates to deep feelings. It involves working with personal *ideals* and *priorities*. Of course, it is necessary first to choose ideals, but then of equal importance is the challenge of maintaining focus and concentration on those same ideals as one moves through life.

You have, no doubt, experienced in your own life the realization that deep feelings are a key ingredient for staying attentive and focused. It is much easier to stay focused on something for which you have strong positive feelings, than it is to concentrate on something dry and lifeless. Just think about the qualitative difference between a moving lecture full of stories which evoke strong positive feelings and an abstract presentation that is only intellectual. Which one is more likely to keep you alert? At which lecture are you more likely to find your attention flitting around the room and away from the speaker?

The ideal you choose is the best focal point to help your one-pointed will to develop. An ideal is a deeply felt motivator for living, not an intellectual abstraction that says "ought" or "should." An ideal invites and holds attention because it evokes reinforcing feelings which make attention more likely to remain in place.

However, as straightforward and simple as all of this may sound, most people have very little capacity to concentrate. You can quickly discover this for yourself just by sitting quietly and trying to focus attention for a few minutes in meditation. But the absence of this quality isn't a problem for meditation alone. Because this quality of will is usually asleep, we experience a wide range of difficulties in life.

Consider, for example, Nathan who is a 45-year-old business executive. Although his life has all the appearance of success, he is still troubled. His excellent salary, beautiful home, and handsome family don't erase the fact that he is plagued by a nagging physical ailment. Nathan has a chronic problem with his digestive system that is diagnosed as nervous bowel and which could easily progress to colitis. His physician can find no physical cause for his ailment, and Nathan was told that it is psychologically produced.

He would probably be surprised to learn that his problem is produced by a failure of his will. It is the farthest thing from his mind that his intestinal difficulties are the indirect result of one quality of his will being asleep. Yet, on careful analysis of his life patterns, this is exactly what can be found.

Nathan finds it extraordinarily hard to keep his attention in the present moment and on what is at hand. He is such a good planner and such an anticipator that he is almost never able to be at peace with the present moment. He usually fails to focus his mind one-pointedly on what he is doing. Even when he is getting something done, another part of him is already off in his imagination anticipating the next task.

Such an orientation to life has made him "productive and successful," but it has also produced a sick body. The key to his problem lies with his will. His body is likely to keep giving him these warning signs. It can get well only when he learns to awaken his will enough to be able to give his attention purposefully in a one-pointed and focused way to the present moment. He must learn to stop allowing it to dance around nervously in an imagined future.

However, a healthy capacity to concentrate and focus should not be confused with the caricature of will at this level. There is an imposter of the will called obsession. It may resemble in many ways one-pointedness and concentration, but it is produced by fear or guilt. It is a bogus, surrogate will that does not lead to a healthy personality.

Obsession has the feature of one-pointedness, but it lacks any capacity to help you see reality more clearly. If you are obsessed with making money, your one-pointedness causes you to distort perception. That obsession is probably produced by insecurity—by fear. With this kind of obsession, your view of everything and everybody is twisted into a picture of how you can make your next profit. If you are obsessed with getting love back from a specific person, it produces a tunnel vision. Your view of life is distorted and all other relationships fade in importance.

But obsessions can lead to neurosis, or even worse to serious mental instability. On the other hand, a healthy, genuine will serves a different function. It brings you closer to an objective view of the world. Real Will frees you to see yourself and others with greater clarity and insight.

7. Synthesis and Harmony

Things don't always fit together nicely. But your will allows you to deal with the fragmentary nature of life in a way that is beyond the realm of logic. The will permits you to respond creatively to the contradictions of living and the paradoxes of human nature. So much of what you face in life and in yourself cannot be dealt with satisfactorily using the three-dimensional laws of logic. Without a healthy will, you may find yourself ineffectively trying to achieve wholeness by cutting out or denying parts of life.

For example, what do you do when confronted with contradictions? How do you deal with your own internal paradoxes? Oftentimes the logical mind cannot see any way to synthesize or harmonize differences. Are you serious *and* fun-loving? Are you generous *and* tight with money? If things are viewed only from a material perspective, then there seems to be no recourse but to deny or repress one side of the polarity.

What happens if you discover that you are *both* a person of deep faith *and* a person who doubts and questions? Your logical mind has trouble synthesizing that sort of difference, and it may try to suppress one side or the other. Or, what happens if you find that you are *both* a person with a great need for others *and* a person who is fiercely independent? How can those equally true and real sides of yourself be integrated?   The will is a faculty of your soul which allows you to disengage from the *familiar* dimension of mind and move to a higher dimension of mind. For example, a three-dimensional, logical mind operates from an assumption of either/or. You can never resolve a paradox or harmonize a polarity from this level of mental functioning.

However, the synthesizing, harmonizing will can move your attention and awareness to a dimension of mind where *inclusive* resolution is possible (i.e., "A *and* B are both true" rather than "Either A or B is true"). A word to describe the *effect* of this act of will is *synergy*. Its meaning is described in the adage "the whole is more than the sum of its parts." In other words, there is a way of synthesizing the parts and fragments of life and creating something of a higher order than before (i.e., a higher amount of energy or higher meaning than would be expected, or even a higher dimension of reality).

Consider the following analogy. It is only a model and makes its point in terms of dimensions. How could we put together these six two-dimensional squares (each of which has only height and width)?

If we think with the logic of only height and width, there are many possibilities, but they all produce something that is of the same two-dimensional order. For example:

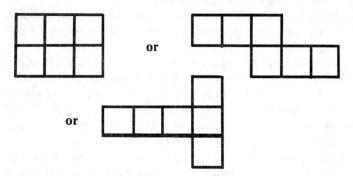

or

or

But what can happen if the will is used to move attention and awareness to a different level of mind. By itself two-dimensional mind would never "think" to become three-dimensional mind, but will's capacity *to disengage from the influences of a mental state* makes this possible. In so doing, a synergistic condition is made possible. The same six squares can be turned into three-dimensional space to create a cube! Parts and fragments which were individually only of two dimensions can be integrated in such a way that the three-dimensional space of height, width, and depth is filled.

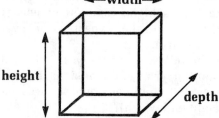

Admittedly, this is a highly abstract analogy, and you may be left to wonder how it relates to your efforts to create greater self-understanding and inner harmony. However, the applicability of the analogy may be clearer if you remember this possibility: As a *soul*, you are of a higher dimensional reality than what logic can analyze. For you to experience harmony and synthesis of the contradictory aspects of your soul, a quality of will is needed. It can awaken you to the higher dimensional aspects of your mind which operate in an intuitive, holistic, and integrative way. If this kind of will is undeveloped or asleep, the likely result is a life full of disharmony, fragmentation, and confusion.

Consider, for example, the case of Joan who is a 25-year-old graduate student in economics. In addition to her interest in business, finance, and economics, she has been on a long search in her personal life for philosophical and spiritual meaning. Yet she has now arrived at a point of great confusion and cynicism. She has run up against what seem to be insurmountable obstacles created by all the contradictions she has found in life. In the field of economics, she has discovered that all the economic systems and strategies which promise universal prosperity contain flaws which are likely to create new problems as they solve old ones. In her spiritual studies it seems to her that every spiritual truth has a complementary but contradictory additional truth. In her search for self-understanding, she has discovered a perplexing paradox about herself. She is a person who wants to be obedient to a higher sense of order and purpose, but she is also a person who needs her personal freedom.

All of these paradoxes and contradictions have left her confused and cynical about the hopes of ever pulling her life together into a meaningful whole. But her difficulty is not really the creation of a faulty world or imperfect reasoning. Her cynical outlook is the result of a failure of will. Only by awakening her will can she disengage from the influences of her present mental condition. Only by awakening her will can she see both the world and herself from a higher dimensional perspective.

To awaken and develop her synthesizing, harmonizing will, Joan must guard against a caricature of this quality: a kind of synthesizing or blending which doesn't produce the "something extra" of synergy. Instead it reduces everything to norms and averages. The imposter, surrogate will (often produced by laziness) attempts to integrate by blurring uniqueness, by homogenizing life. It loses the individuality of each component as it combines. But true synergy is possible because the specialness and distinctiveness of each ingredient part is respected.

Let's look more closely at the difference between these two types of blending. The first type corresponds to impostor will. Imagine that you had three similar bottles of sugar-solution water. The bottles contain solutions of 10%, 20%, and 30% sugar, respectively. If you blend the three in equal quantities, the resultant solution will be an "average" 20% solution. The uniqueness of the three individual components is lost. That is a homogenizing blend that fails to create something bigger.

In contrast, imagine that you play three notes on the piano: C, E, and G. Each note is the sound of a particular rate of vibration, but what is the sound of the three played together as a chord? The chord is not a single tonal sound which averages the three components. It is synergistically "something extra" that is created, while the integrity of the three individual notes still exists simultaneously. That is exactly what is possible when a healthy and awakened will synthesizes and integrates diversities in life. The mind is lifted by the will to a higher mode of operation from which a whole, new view of life is possible. The different notes of life can be experienced as a harmonious chord.

In our example, through a healthy will Joan can escape from her cynicism. As she sees herself and her life from a broader mental outlook, contradictions start to appear as something else. Each pair of polar opposites is a reminder of the richness of life. Each side has its own time and place of rightness, but no single description or theory can capture the whole truth.

A Summary of the Qualities

The table opposite summarizes the ideas we have examined about each of the seven qualities. You can use it as a handy reference for the personal inventory exercise which follows. The position of the qualities in this table, from bottom to top, will make more sense at the end of this chapter.

Quality of will	Characteristics of this quality	Impostor, surrogate will for this quality
Synthesis and harmony	Unifies the fragments of life; "the whole is more than the sum of its parts"	Homogenized blend which blurs uniqueness
One-pointed, focused concentration	Attentiveness, especially in the inner mental realm	Obsession
Decisive, resolute choice	Decision making that goes through three stages with proper timing: confusion, options, choice	Hurried decision making
Patient persistence	Understands the purpose of events; committed to actions for change	Stubbornness; laid-back passivity
Courageous initiative	Lets go of the old and builds new patterns	Recklessness
Discipline and control	Affirms the positive of what needs to be done; flexible and sensitive to immediate situation	Repression
Dynamic and energetic	Taps the universal energy fount; fosters growth and change	"Hyper" or manic

A Personal Inventory

Take time to make these seven qualities of your will more personally meaningful. Think about how you relate to these seven qualities of will. You may want to write down your answers to the questions listed below. These questions are meant to serve as an outline for your inventory and personal assessment. But use the questions merely as a starting point. Feel free to let the self-analysis that is related to a particular quality extend into further issues.

Most likely you will find that your will is more fully awake, operative, and healthy in some of the seven qualities than in others. You may also find that for some of the qualities your real will is not just asleep, but that habit patterns of mind have usurped its role and acted as an imposter, surrogate will.

There may be major differences among the various areas of your life. For example, you may have a healthy self-disciplining will in only one area of your life—daily meditation—but in no other area. You may find that the imposter quality of stubbornness comes up in two principal areas—your relationship with your daughter and your attitudes toward money.

For *each* of the seven qualities, think about these questions concerning your will:

(1) In what areas of your life do you sometimes *success-fully* express this particular quality?

(2) In what areas of your life is this quality almost always asleep?

(3) Where in your life do you see signs of this quality's imposter?

The Chakras as Centers of Will

In many esoteric traditions about human nature, there are seven spiritual centers or chakras. (In ancient Sanskrit language these mean "wheels" because of the wheel-like vortices of energy which clairvoyants claim they can see at each center.) They are located within the physical, etheric, and astral bodies, and they constitute one of the central models of many spiritual and metaphysical systems. There is general agreement about the approximate location of these seven centers in the body and about the qualities of human consciousness and experience to which they relate. These centers are sometimes called "psychic centers" because of the way in which they may relate to the awakening of paranormal perception.

Each center acts like a *transducer*, transmitting influences from more subtle and spiritual dimensions into the denser, more concrete realm of material forms. A transducer is generally understood as a device that takes energy from one system in one form and transmits it to another system in a different form. For example, a telephone serves as a transducer by taking electrical impulses from telephone lines and transmitting them to the human ear in the form of sound.

Not only are the spiritual centers described as mediators for the spiritual life force moving into the human body, but they are also seen as storehouses of karmic habit. That is to say, each chakra is predisposed by conditioning or learned memories to operate in particular ways. For example, the fourth spiritual center relates to the consciousness of human love. Suppose you have mentally built patterns of jealousy and envy with your attitudes and emotions. In this case, your efforts at human love have been distorted and selfish. But where does that habit pattern live? The predisposition may be encoded in the physical brain, but the tendency is stored also in the subtle energy patterns of the fourth chakra as well.

The following chart describes the location of each center and the qualities of consciousness associated with it.

7	**behind the forehead**	oneness; spiritual healing; universal love
6	**top of the head or center of the brain**	higher mind integrating intellect and intuition; the logos
5	**throat**	choice; decision
4	**heart**	human love and sympathy
3	**solar plexus**	the use of force or power in earthly expression

2 lower abdomen	the polarity of yin/yang or feminine/masculine
1 groin or base of spine	survival and nurturance of physical self; survival of the species through reproduction

This chart is merely the sketchiest of outlines. In fact, it fails to note one controversy among the different systems: whether the sixth or seventh center should be designated as the "third eye" behind the forehead. However, with this basic chart in mind, it is possible to proceed with a look at how the seven qualities of will just described are *related to the seven centers*. Some systems of thought have suggested that *only* the fifth center is related to the will—that, in fact, it is *the* will center. However, if we keep in mind these two points, it would seem to make more sense that *all* the chakras are will centers:

(1) The nature of the will is far broader than just choice and decision making.

(2) The chakras are *consciousness centers* and consciousness is the product of mind *and* will in interaction.

The following column might, therefore, be added to the chakra chart above. The seven qualities you have explored in this chapter were presented in a numerical order to correspond to the seven centers:

7 **Synthesis and harmony,** which helps you attain *oneness*

6 **Focused, one-pointedness,** which characterizes the *higher mind*

5 **Decisiveness,** which allows you to *choose*

4 **Patient persistence,** which is required in *human loving*

3 **Courageous initiative,** which expresses your *power* to effect change in material life

2 **Discipline and control,** which allows the *poles* of yin and yang to be *balanced*

1 Energetic, dynamic living, which allows you to have the resources to *survive*

Anyone who is working with the chakras model as a tool for meditation can see the value of this additional column. It suggests the very qualities which must be awakened in order to deepen the meditative experience. Or, anyone who is accustomed to seeing challenges in terms of which spiritual center is engaged can also find a helpful tool here. Identifying the specific quality of will most involved may reveal a key to solving the problem.

The notion of seven qualities of the will is an extraordinarily useful one. It brings the will from an abstract, metaphysical concept into the immediacy of daily living. It allows each of us to see where relative strengths and weaknesses lie. Nevertheless, it does not offer a *developmental sequence* for growth and maturity of will. Different people develop the seven qualities in different orders. However, a progressive series of stages for will development is described in the next chapter.

RECOMMENDED ADDITIONAL READING

"The Qualities of Will" in *The Act of Will*, Roberto Assagioli (Penguin Books, Baltimore, 1973)

The creator of the psychosynthesis approach deals specifically with the will in its many aspects. Of special importance are sections on the seven qualities of will described in the chapter cited above.

"The Will" in *What We May Be*, Piero Ferrucci (Tarcher Press, Los Angeles, 1982)

Written by a professional practitioner of psychosynthesis methods, this book is a well-written, applicable outline of how to awaken personal and transpersonal potentials. It has a noteworthy chapter directly concerning the will.

"The Physiology of Meditation" in *Meditation and the Mind of Man,* Herbert Puryear and Mark Thurston (A.R.E. Press, Virginia Beach, Va., 1975)

"What Happens in Our Bodies When We Meditate" in *The Inner Power of Silence,* Mark Thurston (Inner Vision, Virginia Beach, Va., 1986)

A chapter in each of these two books deals in detail with the seven spiritual centers and the qualities of consciousness associated with each center.

Mysticism, Evelyn Underhill (Dutton, New York, 1910)

This book is truly one of the classics in the field of Christian mysticism. Of special note are the two chapters on "introversion," which is Underhill's term for meditation.

CHAPTER FOUR

Stages in Developing Your Will

How can you develop your will? With a clearer view of what the will is, you may still be left with the question of how it can grow and expand effectively. Having seen some of its characteristics and qualities, you may still need a strategy for awakening the capabilities which the will promises.

In Chapter 5 you can explore and apply a set of specific *training exercises* for the will. However, in this chapter a more fundamental set of ideas is presented. Within yourself you can observe will development. That is to say, your will goes through distinct stages of evolution as it awakens within you.

The concept of developmental stages is familiar to many fields of study. For example, mathematics has a time-tested curriculum in which the student is led through a series of developmental steps in knowledge. First, the student learns to count and then to add and subtract. Only after these fundamentals are mastered can the student move on to multiplication, division, and fractions. Later, mathematical subjects such as algebra can be added, as well as the more advanced topics like calculus. Each new stage builds upon the previous one.

But does the same kind of neat, systematic sequence apply to the building blocks of the human soul: spirit, mind, and will? If the component called spirit is thought of in terms of the fundamental, unified *energy* of the universe, then the scientific model of vibratory rates demonstrates distinct stages. Ranging from extremely low frequency radio waves to the highest frequency x-rays, at least one kind of orderly, sequential expression of energy exists.

Perhaps even more suggestive of developmental stages is the way the human mind can be experienced. Many psychological theories and models refer to layers of mental activity, only one of which is the familiar mental state of conscious thinking and perceiving. As awareness moves to mental regions which are most frequently unconscious, then more expansive states of mind are available. It may be like peeling layers of an onion; and as awareness moves deeper and deeper into the psyche, then higher dimensional expressions of mind are possible. A simple way of describing a developmental, growth sequence for mind expansion is: first, the conscious mind; then, the subconscious mind; and finally, the superconscious mind. Of course, there may be substages as well as traps where the developmental unfolding can get stymied.

Anyone who has tried to meditate knows how true this is. As you begin to quiet the normal, conscious mind and seek contact with the superconscious mind, what happens? You begin to contact material from your subconscious mind. At first, it may be recent thoughts and memories that have not been tucked away for long. As you become more quiet and focused in meditation, deeper elements of your subconscious may pop into your awareness. How easy it is to get distracted by all of this! How readily the true goal of the meditation periods gets stymied as you become caught up in these mental digressions!

However, remember that there are not three different minds, but instead three distinct ways that the oneness of mind can be experienced. We must not be misled at this point, as we think about any kind of developmental stages. For example, there is a oneness to the law of mathematics, and multiplication tables and algebraic laws are two different ways of experiencing mathematics. In a similar fashion, a five-stage sequence of will development (soon to be described) does *not* refer to five different wills. Instead, there is a oneness of will within your soul, but there are growth steps in how you can experience it.

The classic three-stage model of mind development (as described above) has at least one important difference from the example of a mathematical curriculum. In learning mathematics, the student cannot expect to have any (even momentary) experiences out of the prescribed curriculum order. While learning multiplication the student cannot expect to have temporary "leaps ahead" momentarily to grasp calculus theory. However, such leaps can and do happen within the developmental stages of the mind (and within the stages of will development to be described shortly). For example, a visionary experience may give you a temporary glimpse of the superconscious mind. Or, a spontaneous psychic experience may give you a momentary taste of certain aspects of the subconscious mind. The stages are, therefore, not rigid but contain a certain measure of flexibility. *You can expect to experience advanced stages of mind or will, but should not count on being able to maintain them until the previous stages are mastered.*

What, then, would a developmental sequence for will look like? In the curriculum of will growth, what corresponds to learning mathematical addition, or algebra, or calculus?

Since the metaphor of "awakening the will" has frequently been used in previous chapters, perhaps a good starting point would be to examine how the very process of awakening in the morning has stages which build upon each other. Imagine that you are in bed asleep, a stage where no degree of awakening has yet taken place. Suppose that on this particular morning you won't be jarred awake by an alarm clock, but instead you can gradually awaken at your familiar time.

The first stage of awakening is the hypnopompic state in which the inner world of your dreams is mixed with hazy, diffuse perception of the physical environment in your bedroom. In this half-sleep state you are not clear about where you are. This stage may last for seconds or many minutes. Following this, a distinctly different stage emerges in which you become a little more awakened. At this next stage, you are "back in your body"—you come back to your sense of personality and may lazily entertain disjointed, vague thoughts about last night's dreams or what's coming up in the day ahead. But in this stage of wakefulness you probably still find it hard to get out of bed.

Next, your wakefulness can increase to a stage where you feel the desire to be up and to get started on the day. This stage of wakefulness is sufficient for such early morning tasks as washing your face or putting bread in the toaster. However, you probably aren't sufficiently awake at this stage to do things like balance your checkbook or other challenges which require sustained and alert attention. Only later in the morning routine do you realize you've fully awakened and that you are ready to tackle most any task. In this last stage you are as fully awake as you will become during the course of a day.

These steps are presented *not* as the stages of will development, but rather as an *analogy* of how an awakening process progresses through levels and degrees. The will has its own distinctive characteristics for each stage of development; and, like getting up in the morning, each stage builds upon mastery of previous stages.

In psychological and spiritual literature dealing with the will, little attention has been given to any sort of progressive development through stages. Assagioli discusses "aspects" of the will (as a topic separate from his seven "qualities") but makes no attempt to link the aspects into a systematic growth sequence. Other systems have proposed a conscious and an unconscious will, but without a clear description of progressive steps in awakening and harmonizing the two.

But a new understanding of will development is possible. The remainder of this chapter describes a multistage model. This is likely to be a somewhat complex theory which requires careful reading and serious thought about human psychology.

This model of the stages of will has five steps which are sequentially numbered from 0 to 4. The number 0 is chosen for a starting point because it accurately describes the amount of will present at its starting point for growth. As you read the description for each stage, you are likely to recognize that parts of your daily living seem to fit particular stages. In other words, you are probably *not at any single stage* in the development of your will. Instead you may find that one stage of will development clearly defines how you interact in certain relationships and situations, whereas a different stage better describes how you use your will in response to other circumstances. Unfortunately, most of us have very few parts of life where stages 1 through 4 are applied frequently. The most common human responses of life come from stage 0 of will development, so that level invites our immediate attention.

Stage 0: The Sleeping Will

Your will typically exists in a sleeping or unconscious state. You and all those you encounter are, for the most part, walking around through life "asleep." In other words, that which is most essentially real and true about you as a spiritual being is in an unconscious state, largely because of the unawakened state of your will.

The principle is most clearly described by distinguishing between two levels of your being: your *personality* and your *individuality*. These terms were introduced in Chapter 2. Your personality is the acquired set of habit patterns with which you most often operate in life. Your personality traits have largely been learned from parents, teachers, television, etc. They are made up of countless mechanical ways in which you think, feel, and act in the world. In other words, your personality is your familiar sense of identity, but it exists by habit and routine.

Your personality is reactive. In an automatic and very predictable way, it responds to the events of physical life. For example, if someone says something distasteful to you, your personality responds like a machine with automatic thoughts, feelings, and behaviors. No real will is involved, any more than your automobile "wills" to start its engine when you turn the ignition key. Some of the responses of your personality are "nice" and some "not so nice." However, what *all* these automatic reactions have in common is their lack of conscious, willed selection. You are "asleep" in your personality—that is "asleep" to your real identity.

But as individuality, you are a being of will. When you are aware of and identify with individuality, you are able to make choices and be creative. Of course, your individuality is not a perfect self, because it needs to grow and evolve itself. From the level of individuality you are an unfolding spiritual being. This is the identity that is capable of growth, whereas your personality exists to repeat patterns and largely stay the same.

Often it isn't easy to distinguish influences of your individuality from those of your personality. Part of the problem comes from the fact that the personality contains many subpersonalities. Each one is a role that you occasionally play in life, a particular sense of "I" with which you identify. (Recall the example of Janet in Chapter 2.) Because every subpersonality conforms to the characteristics of personality in general, each separate "I" is relatively devoid of will. On the one hand you may notice that your various subpersonalities seem to have separate and conflicting "wills," but on closer examination what looks like will is actually the surrogate will of ingrained habit trying to repeat itself.

Each subpersonality has its own set of habitual ways of thinking, feeling, and acting. Each one also thinks of itself as the "whole show" whenever it is "on stage" (i.e., each has the momentary attention of consciousness). Each subpersonality may try to be sincere; but because of the constantly shifting sense of which "I" you are, it is difficult for you to be consistent in life.

For example, suppose that, at 6:00 p.m., you are reading a book about meditation which deeply inspires you. At that moment, the subpersonality that has your attention, the "I" you think yourself to be, is one which could be labeled "the enthusiastic seeker." In that role you say to yourself, "I'm going to get really serious about meditation and even start getting up at 3:00 a.m. to have a daily meditation period." That aspect of your personality really means it. But in the moment of making such a vow, that subpersonality has forgotten that it is not the whole story of who you are. So, 3:00 a.m. comes, the alarm goes off, but now it is not "the enthusiastic seeker" that rolls over in bed to turn off the alarm. It is a personal sense of identity that might be "the exhausted parent." The planned meditation period doesn't happen.

Whether or not you can personally relate to *this* particular example is not important. No doubt you can think of several examples that *are* relevant from your own life. They are instances in which a shifting sense of personal identity results in intentions not being followed.

The Human Personality as a Wheel

A visual image may help you get a clearer sense of what is meant by the personality. Consider the metaphor of a wheel. If you are on the rim of a rotating wheel, you get the feeling of movement toward a goal, but in the end the wheel merely brings you back to the point from which you began. In the same fashion, your personality may often appear to lead you in new directions only to bring you back to the same issues or problems in life.

To help illustrate this further, think of a time in your life when you wanted to make a change in order to get away from a troublesome person or condition. Perhaps it was a situation in which you could not see your own role in the creation of the problem and tended to blame others, so you wanted out. Perhaps your example relates to a job or a close personal relationship.

Did the change actually solve the problem? Most likely you experienced temporary relief from the difficulty, only to discover months or years later that the same kind of issue or problem was arising again in the new situation, job, or relationship. Because something in you had not been changed, you were drawn back to a similar difficulty. Because your habitual personality was responsible, at least in part, for the creation of the original problem, it was again involved in the creation of the repeated difficulty. Since your personality was controlling your behavior, there was a strong tendency to repeat the past. In this sense we can say that your personality is like a rotating wheel: It moves apparently in a direction away from an old situation, only to bring you back later to the same point from which you began.

In the analogy of the wheel, many subpersonalities live on the rim. Each of these subpersonalities creates a particular feeling of personal identity. In the course of day, your attention moves from one to the next in rather random order. What governs the shift from one sense of identity to the next are the events of daily living: what people say to you, what happens to the stock market, the weather, etc. We could think of these influences which arise from outer, material life as being like pushes which keep the wheel turning. You may recall the experience of helping a child enjoy a merry-go-round on a playground. With the child seated on the merry-go-round and you standing alongside it, you would have to give the rim of the merry-go-round a brief shove every five or ten seconds to keep it turning. Material life gives you those pushes. They prod you from one feeling of who you are to another and, in so doing, keep your wheel turning.

In the diagram below, the subpersonalities are represented by the various "I's" on the rim of the wheel. Each "I" has associated with it a set of spokes. These spokes represent habitual traits which are a part of that particular "I" and its way of seeing and responding to the world. For example, if one of your subpersonalities could be labeled "the compulsive pleaser," you might find that certain attitudes, emotions, and behaviors manifest in an automatic, mechanical way whenever that subpersonality has your attention. The spokes might be labeled with words like "inferiority feelings" or "volunteers for tasks I don't have time to do" or "smiles a lot although it's not sincere," and so forth. Or, if another of your subpersonalities was labeled "the get-it-done administrator," the spokes might have labels like "feeling hurried" or "talks brusquely to subordinates" or "logically categorizes each experience."

The question you face in the development of your will is this: If I am identified with my personality wheel in some part of my life, how can I change, how can I awaken my will enough to resist the mechanical, habitual reactions that are so familiar? The movement from Stage 0 to Stage 1 is frequently motivated by one of the self-centered drives of the personality. Often it is ambition or pride. Some times it is the desire to escape the emotional or physical pain which is continually being re-created by the personality. But whatever the impulse, the first small awakenings are the beginning of a more objective consciousness of life. These initial stirrings of will create the opportunity to shape one's own sense of identity and begin the shift from knowing self as personality to knowing self as individuality.

Stage 1: Negating Will

The first awakenings of will are not very mature expressions. They may be like a child trying to grow up, whose first efforts at adult approaches to life may look awkward. The first stage of will development is merely the capacity to say "no," to set limits by negating, even to use so-called willpower to repress what is undesirable.

How awakened is your will? If you are at Stage 0 of development, with little or no will awakened, then from this highly subjective state you have surrendered all control to your mind. Your actions in life are really re-actions based on habit. Your sense of personal identity in any moment is determined fully by material life conditions and what they stir up in you. But if your will is active, there may be some genuine choice in your action and in your sense of who you are.

It all begins with Stage 1: the initial awakenings of will. Here we find the beginnings of self-reflection. At Stage 1, you start to feel that your personal identity is not necessarily equivalent to what your mind is presenting at the current moment. You begin to distinguish your self-identity (i.e., "Who am I?") from the emotions and attitudes that flood automatically into your awareness. As elementary as this may sound, most of us spend very little of the day with the will awakened to even this first stage.

Instead, we tend to remain "asleep," allowing the habitual mind to totally shape who we feel ourselves to be. If you doubt this, observe yourself carefully for a day, even for an hour. You may notice how often your sense of "I" changes without your having chosen to do so. You may notice how automatic most of your actions are.

This first degree of awakening is not easy. It is a tenuous hold that we first have upon this birthright called the will. Because the movement out of sleep is so difficult, the early awakenings of will are rather crude and even negative in character. But isn't this true of most beginnings? Our early efforts to walk were awkward and poorly controlled; our initial attempts to feed ourselves were messy. In a similar way, the first stage of will development is a sort of negative will: the capacity to say "no." For this reason we might label this stage of will "negating will."

Will, at the first stage, attempts to forge a new sense of personal identity by rejecting the impressions presented by the mind. It takes on a variety of appearances: rebellion, negation, even the Victorian "willpower" or the capacity to reject temptations.

To put another label on this stage of development, we might call it "adolescent will"—not because it is uniquely characteristic of teenagers, but because the images of the young person trying to form his or her new sense of identity apart from parents and family illustrates well the process. Imagine a 15-year-old boy who is getting dressed up to go out on a date. He puts on his brown suit and grey tie, only to have his mother come in and loudly demand that he change to his brown tie. We all know what typically follows. Even if the boy inwardly recognizes that his mother is "right," it is more important to him that the newly emerging integrity of his own personhood be respected. Using Stage 1 will, he rebels; he says "no" to her demands. Here the will has been used to distinguish his own needs and identity from what his mind presents to him: the sights and sounds of his mother, and the memories of his past childhood where she was the authority.

With Stage 1 will, there is a quality of repression inherent in negating the influences from the mind. If Stage 1 is followed by further will development, this sort of repression can be healthy because it allows the experience of a clear feeling of unique personhood. However, if you never go any further than "willpower," such repression is likely to be detrimental. Stage 1 is a positive step in the use of the will to the extent that it allows you to disidentify from patterns of mind that have been controlling your sense of personal identity and your responses to life. This kind of negating allows you to stand apart from old patterns of mind and create a new sense of yourself.

We all have personally meaningful expressions of how first-stage will manifests in our lives. For one person, it is that which says, "I am not going to eat another piece of that pie which my mind is telling me would taste very good." For another person, it is that which says, "I am not going to give in to that old feeling of resentment which my mind is telling me is the justifiable way to react to this individual." An effective self-observation exercise for each of us is to watch for the ways in which these stirrings of will awaken and manifest in our lives.

Stages 1, 2 and 3 of will development can be seen in terms of a healthy/unhealthy polarity. If the will gets distorted at a particular stage and takes on the unhealthy side of the polarity, then further growth of will is blocked. However, by taking care to maintain a balanced, healthy expression of will at a particular stage, progress on to the next stage is possible.

For Stage 1 of will, the unhealthy pole is the "doubting cynic." If you get caught up in only saying "no" to things with this level of will and never use it to affirm by saying "yes," then cynicism is the result. A person stuck at this level is often stubborn and full of resentments and doubt.

On the other hand, a Stage 1 will can be healthy and be "the affirmer of individuality." It permits you to feel your creative uniqueness. It can allow you to experience your independence and freedom to be self-determining.

Often the key to keeping Stage 1 will healthy is to maintain a sense of hope and optimism about life. This kind of basic trust in the goodness of oneself, others, and the universe is a powerful aid in combating cynicism. Hope allows you to use will, not only to say "no" to things, but also to say "yes" and affirm a positive vision for your life.

Stage 2: Skillful Will

The will awakened to its second stage is more than just an intensification of qualities from the first stage. On the one hand, the second stage is characterized by a greater degree of self-reflection; but added to this are distinct new ways in which the individual feels his or her own identity and reacts to life.

What is meant by self-reflection? It is not merely preoccupation with oneself. Instead, it is self-criticism—not the guilt-producing kind of accusations we might think of—but more like the objective view of a literary critic. Self-reflection is the capacity to achieve an inner split so that a part of oneself goes on with the familiar thoughts, feelings, and actions, while another part observes. Stated poetically, it is a matter of "standing aside and watching self go by." At the second stage of will development, the capacity for such self-reflection is strengthened.

More important, the second stage is characterized by the ability to *blend and synthesize*. At Stage 1, the integrity of one's individuality was maintained by rejecting and negating certain impressions received from the mind (whether the source of these impressions was internal or external). At Stage 2 the sense of individuality has grown stronger, and it is possible to use will to reconnect with the inner and outer worlds presented by the mind.

The second stage might be labeled "adult will," again not so much because all adults demonstrate this development, but because our idealized notion of what it means to be adult-like includes characteristics bestowed by this level of the will. The adult is expected to be able to create skillfully a blend of two factors:

1. An inner knowledge of what one's own unique individuality wants and needs in the present moment.

2. The vast array of influences coming from other people, the environment, and one's own attitudinal and emotional past.

At Stage 1 of the will, differences between these two factors were resolved by the second factor being rejected in favor of the first. But now a new means of resolution is possible. "Adult will" skillfully blends the genuine needs coming from one's own individuality with the demands and expectations arising from what the mind perceives.

What does the voice of Stage 2 will say within you? How does it feel? Take the example of being tempted to eat another piece of pie. Stage 1 negating will would use will-power, repressively saying "no" to the memory of how good pie tastes and the desire immediately to repeat the experience. However, Stage 2 skillful will might express itself as, "I know that pie would taste good and I am going to have some—but not right now—at the appropriate time."

Or, consider the case of the 15-year-old who is told by his mother to switch to the brown tie. We might expect that, when a similar event occurs ten years after this time, the now 25-year-old adult would respond differently to his mother. Because his will is more awakened and he has a stronger, less vulnerable contact with his own unique personhood, he can skillfully blend the factors present. He might say, "Mother, you are right, that brown tie would look good with this suit. Next time I wear this suit, I think I will wear it. But tonight I am going to go ahead with what I think looks just as good."

Admittedly, these examples are a bit simplistic. Often life offers challenges with much more complex issues in which pat answers don't work. But the principle remains the same in any situation we confront. There is a level of the will from which we can operate that does not require us to be stubborn or negative in affirming our sense of individuality. No doubt, there are times when Stage 1 will is the more appropriate stage from which to operate, but often the appropriateness is because of our own needs for development and growth—and not so much something inherent in the event. From time to time in our lives, we need to cycle back to Stage 1. It is not a developmental step which is reserved for teenagers. In fact, if you carefully observe yourself, you shall likely see that in a typical day your will awakens and falls back to sleep many times. You probably see that you spend most of the day at Stage 0, some time at Stage 1 and only brief peak moments at Stage 2.

Another label for Stage 2 will is the "redeeming, nurturant will." With your sense of unique personhood and individuality established by Stage 1 will, it is possible to go back and re-embrace those patterns of mind which you negated and repressed at Stage 1. In this fashion there is an archetypically feminine quality to Stage 2 will, in contrast to the active—even harsh—character of the more masculine Stage 1 will.

The "redeeming, nurturant will" is able to direct attention so as to find, within the patterns of mind previously rejected, something which is judged good. For example, the 25-year-old young man can now use Stage 2 will to re-embrace his mother's criticism. He can recognize some aspect of her criticism with which he can agree. Stage 1 will has made him strong in his sense of individuality, and now he need not fear being overwhelmed by memories of his childhood and mother's authority. He is able to use Stage 2 will to find the essence of caring within his mother's behavior and respond to it rather than to the strident form her criticism takes.

Just as there was a healthy/unhealthy polarity at Stage 1 (i.e., affirmer of individuality/negating cynic), there is a corresponding polarity for Stage 2. A distorted form of will at this level is the "compromiser of integrity." If you start finding a place for everything without any regard for the ideals of your individuality, then what was gained at Stage 1 is forfeited and you get blocked at Stage 2. If your guiding principle is to compromise to avoid a struggle or discord, then you have slipped out of a genuinely skillful use of your will.

The healthy side of Stage 2 is the "synergistic integrator." Recall the meaning of "synergy." (It was the key to the seventh quality of will in Chapter 3.) With the healthy side of this stage, timings exist for the contradictions of life— but always guided by a clear sense of your own individual integrity and ideal. You find yourself integrating the fragmentary, competing demands in life so that the principle of synergy is demonstrated. You experience how the whole is more than the sum of its parts.

What helps to keep your will healthy at Stage 2? An acceptance of the contradictory, paradoxical nature of life. Because spiritual reality is of a higher dimension than physical life, higher truth often manifests as paradoxical opposites. For example, since you are a being of greater dimension than the three-dimensional physical world, you have within you many contradictory sides—all of which have their own measure of validity. The same fact holds true of any person you encounter. Although your logical mind has trouble with paradoxes and would prefer to have truth just one way or the other, an understanding of the paradoxical nature of life can help you see the role that can be played by a healthy, skillful will. It may be easier to use the will at Stage 1 to repress certain sides of yourself. It may be easier to use negating will to say "no" to certain aspects of other people. It shows a real development of will to use it skillfully and find ways to balance and unify the many sides of life.

Stage 3: Empowering Will

A dramatic change takes place with the third level of development. Up until now, the relationship between mind and will has had a consistent character. The mind has been the "senior partner" in the pair. Now the will awakens sufficiently so that the balance begins to shift.

We can label this stage of development "empowering will"—something quite different from "willpower." With the will awakened to this third step, you recognize that no influence of mind is stronger than the will. The feeling which is created says, "I am an identity—a being—that is quite independent of anything my mind may present to me for experiencing." With this recognition comes a tremendous sense of control and power over life.

This stage of development is demonstrated in a particularly effective manner by the experience of a lucid dream, which was already mentioned in Chapter 2. Recall that this curious phenomenon consists of the awareness that you are in a dream *while the dream is still going on.* It is a fairly rare occurrence for most dreamers, but one that is not easily forgotten because of its novelty and great impact. The term "lucid dream" has frequently been misunderstood to imply any dream that is especially clear; for example, one in which the symbols are straightforward and transparent, for a dream in which the interpretation is literally given while one is still in the dream. However significant those kinds of dream examples may be, they do not describe lucid dreams. Rather the term is used strictly for a special event that occasionally happens in our dreams: the recognition of dreaming while the dream is still going on.

What do such lucid dreams have to do with the will? In a typical (i.e., non-lucid) dream, you are in a highly subjective state, with little or no will present. Even the dream experiences in which you seem to be making choices are probably more a matter of unconscious habit patterns, with mind doing the choosing. There is virtually no self-reflection or recognition of your sense of individuality. But something very different takes place in a lucid dream: The will awakens.

With the introduction of lucidity, you recognize that you have identity and individuality apart from the dream events. In saying, "This is merely a dream state," what are you the dreamer actually asserting? You recognize that this dream world is somehow distinct from the normal world of physical life. For example, consider this actual lucid dream:

> I'm in a dark, poor section of a city. A young man starts chasing me down an alley. In the dream, I'm running for what seems to be a long time. Then I become aware that I am dreaming and that much of my dream life is spent running from male pursuers. I say to myself, "I'm tired of this never-ending chase." I stop running, turn around and walk up to the man. I touch him and say, "Is there anything I can do to help you?" He becomes very gentle and open to me and replies, "Yes. My friend and I need help." I go to the apartment they share and talk with them both about their problems, feeling compassionate love for them both. (*Lucid Dreaming* by Scott Sparrow, A.R.E. Press)

In this dream, self-reflection awakens sufficiently so that the dreamer (a woman in this case) recognizes an identity apart from the image which her mind is presenting in the dream. In a typical dreaming state, she would have responded subjectively to the events of the dream. She probably would have run or fought. The outer dream events would have shaped her identity as a pursued, fearful person. But with lucidity, the will acts potently to create a sense of individuality which differs from the influences from the dream. From this new feeling of identity, she responds in a creative, loving fashion; and, in return, the images of mind (i.e., the dream symbols of the men) alter their behavior and attitude.

This dream beautifully illustrates an effective use of will at the first and second stages, and then it concludes with will at the third stage: "empowering will." With the awareness and words, "I'm tired of this never-ending chase," the dreamer exhibits Stage 1 will by *negating* old mental patterns. With the decision to turn, confront, and embrace that which was previously avoided and negated, the dreamer demonstrates the skillful, redeeming, nurturant will of Stage 2. Then, at the third level, mind becomes the servant of will, as demonstrated in the dream when the images and events change.

Oftentimes, however, empowering will is not used in such a constructive manner. In fact, this third stage of development is a critical, even dangerous, point. The possibility and temptation arise to use the will to serve selfish or limited ends. In a lucid dream, the tendency is to use the new-found power of awakened will to manipulate the dream content. Such experiences are quite possible and available with this level of will. Most people who have had lucid dreams have discovered such remarkable capabilities. They find that they can escape from uncomfortable dream images by just flying away, or by wishing or willing the undesirable images of mind to change into something else.

In the example quoted above, the woman might have used her lucidity in a less constructive way. She could have turned to her pursuers and used her will to imagine them as friends or benevolent beings. No doubt, such dream manipulation would have taken place. But in doing so she would have avoided something within her in need of healing—it would have been disrespect for the integrity of the dream. Admittedly, the dream images did change once her lucidity emerged. However, it was not because she tried to overwhelm the dream images with the power of her will. Instead, she used the power of her will to create a constructive, fear-free sense of her own identity, and then the dream began to change as a natural result.

What, we might ask, does all this have to do with daily living? The answer is that the process experienced in a lucid dream is very similar to what is possible in physical conscious life. We can learn "lucid living." It may not be experienced in daily life exactly in the way it is in the dream state. However, both involve the awakening of the will to this stage we call "empowering will."

When the empowering will emerges, a fundamental shift in perception takes place. In the dream state, the perceptual shift creates the view that "this is only a dream" and, therefore, a feeling of invulnerability. In physical life, the perceptual shift creates the view that the world presented by the physical, conscious mind is actually the past and not the present.

This recognition is a radical change in how we view life. At this third stage, not only has the balance of influence shifted from the mind to the will, but now the mind is experienced as primarily an agent of the past. A careful analysis shows that this, in fact, makes sense, even though it is contrary to the way in which we are accustomed to seeing things.

Your attitudes and emotions are patterns of mind which merely reflect your past experiences. When you feel angry or jealous, the emotional experience is largely determined by past events. The anger you may feel today is real; but its energy has been patterned and formed by circumstances in your past.

But not only are the internal attitudes and emotions recognized as being of the past, we recognize that the external, physical world is the past also. On the one hand,

this notion sounds nonsensical. But consider the
implications of the universal law, "The spirit is the life,
mind is the builder, and the physical is the result." That law
simply states that everything which we experience as
physical reality (e.g., our bodies, material objects, etc.) has
been created first at the dimension where mind is the
builder. Initially mind creates, and then later (perhaps
seconds later or perhaps years later) the pattern of energy
manifests in physical form. The findings of psychosomatic
medicine illustrate this law very well as it relates to our
physical bodies. Through your state of mind you build the
relative health or dis-ease of your body. Your body is a
concrete, material expression of your past. The law works
in a similar fashion for other objects or events we
experience as physical reality.

The awakening of your will at the third stage—
empowering will—brings this recognition: Your mind no
longer has such a hold on you because you realize that the
impressions brought to you by your mind are images and
influences of the past. They *are real*, but your tendency up
until now has been to misinterpret them and to give them an
unwarranted control in shaping your own sense of who you
are. Even with this level of awakening, the mind still
functions as the builder, but it is as the servant-builder
under the direction of the will. At this third stage your will
is an initiator, directing the building of new patterns by
your mind.

But if mind is that which gives you impressions of the
past, then what is the present? Your inner response. Your
sense of who you are in the situation. For example, suppose
you are at a dinner party and someone makes an insulting
remark to you across the table. If you are metaphorically
asleep, at Stage 0 of will, then you react in a subjective way.
Your inner sense of who you are is determined by whatever
emotional pattern arises from your subconscious mind in
response to what you have just heard. You may toss a
similar insult back.

But if you have awakened your will to Stage 1, you resist
the inner emotional pattern and have the "willpower" to
keep silent. At Stage 2 you find something to say or do

which skillfully blends an appreciation for the other person's dislike for you along with the clear awareness that your real identity is not what the insulting remark implied. Perhaps this would be a good-humored comment which takes note of the feeling behind the other person's attack but, at the same time, proposes a different picture of who you are. It skillfully invites your antagonist to see you in a new way.

However, with the third stage of will development another option in this story is introduced. With empowering will, you recognize that the feelings and comments of the other person are actually images of his or her past. What you are seeking and hearing is not really the present of that soul, but rather a physical expression of experiences from the past. You also recognize that your own emotional reactions of outrage and resentment are patterns of energy arising from your own past. All of this is quite real, and yet the will allows your awareness to be in the actual present moment. The will allows you to choose your identity—to be your real individuality. Then, whatever response you do make can be creative and can represent the best in you.

To depict this in a diagram, notice that the mind tends to draw you back to the past. Even its building and creating function has the *tendency* to re-create and reinforce patterns from the past. When the will is awakened, it draws you into the future. *When your will is in charge and creatively directing your mind, movement toward your destiny is possible.*

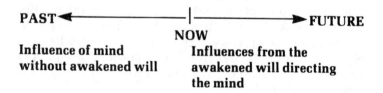

PAST ◄───────────|───────────► FUTURE
NOW

Influence of mind   Influences from the
without awakened will   awakened will directing
                           the mind

In the example above, Stage 3 will is described in a

healthy mode. However, it doesn't always work that way. As one is empowered by will, that power is not always used constructively. The third stage of will development is a potentially dangerous one. Particularly at this level the will can be used to fulfill selfish aims rather than altruistic ones. With the sense of personal power it provides, you can literally lead yourself astray. Without a spiritual purpose to keep yourself directed, the influence of the will over the mind can get you even more deeply entrapped in a mistaken identity for yourself.

For example, consider again the moment you become lucid in a dream. How is your will used in this opportune situation? As already mentioned, some lucid dreams practice a form of dream manipulation. The will is used to wish things which have been desired but unfulfilled in daily life (e.g., having a dream imagery affair with a sexually desirable person who is unobtainable in waking life). However, this may not be a wise decision. Such dream manipulation using empowering will creates patterns of mind which do not dissolve upon awakening from the dream. Such inner behavior is as unsound for personal ecology as is tossing trash from one's car window, thinking to be rid of it. There is a more appropriate way to deal with unwanted trash, just as there are better ways to deal with desires and fantasy needs.

Stage 3 is the danger zone of will development because one can misunderstand this level, believing it to be the final step, the goal. If you don't feel something still ahead—the transcendent—there is the temptation to use the power of this level to strengthen the desire patterns of your personality. Furthermore, a person who has awakened will to this level can have a remarkable influence over those other people who have not yet awakened the will, especially those who spend most of their time at Stage 0 sleep.

One of the best and most tragic examples of this stage is the life of Adolph Hitler. By all accounts of him, it seems that this man had profoundly developed his will and along with it a very distinct sense of his own identity. That will was able to withstand many forms of resistance to his chosen identity in the early years of his rise to power. But in that rise, he seemed to have an almost hypnotic effect on the minds of others. Not only was Hitler's own mind the servant of his will, but the minds of others became servants, too.

Although you are not likely to misuse Stage 3 will to the extent Hitler did, you should recognize the potentials of an unhealthy side of this developmental stage. This side of the polarity can be labeled the "egomaniac manipulator" because of the way it allows a very limited self-definition to control one's own mind, as well as those of others. This kind of *willfulness* blocks growth and makes impossible a transition to the highest stage of will.

In contrast, the healthy side of Stage 3 will can be labeled the "Wizard Alchemist." It gives the image of almost magical powers working for a positive purpose. The alchemy we want is not the superficial kind which manipulates lead into gold. Instead, real alchemy is inner work to transform us spiritually.

Good will is what is required if this third stage is to be a stepping-stone to the next stage. Without an ideal of goodness coupled to empowering will, we cannot hope to grow further. If good will is extended to include the characteristic of humility, then you have the key to the healthy side of will at this stage. In other words, if you adopt a humble attitude of *willingness* instead of willfulness, then a movement to Stage 4 is possible.

It is our opportunity and our destiny to develop fully the empowering will at a personal level. Spiritual growth requires the complete empowerment of the individual life. Only then can we take the next and biggest step.

Stage 4: Transpersonal Will

Stage 4 is the Real Will of the soul, what might also be called the "transpersonal will." In traditional religion this has often been referred to as the will of God. The two points of view are not incompatible because at this level the individual's will has aligned itself with the will of God.

Surrender is required of you in order to move from Stage 3 to Stage 4. What must be given up is the extensive personal power created by empowering will. You must also surrender a certain sense of your own identity, which up until now has still maintained a high degree of separateness from the whole. It is not that Stage 4 makes you return to the oceanic feeling of oneness which you had as an infant. It is not a loss of unique individuality. Instead, it is a surrender in which your old, mistaken notion of personal identity dies and what is resurrected is your authentic identity—your individuality. That individuality knows itself to be itself (i.e., full self-reflection) and simultaneously knows itself as one with the universe.

A subtle point is often misunderstood about surrender, death, and rebirth. The personality-self is relieved to hear that in moving from Stage 3 to Stage 4, unique personhood is not destroyed. But the personality-self assumes mistakenly that it shall be the identity that stays most important. To the contrary, the personality loses its primary place. What is awakened is something resembling the personality in that it knows its own distinct nature. However, this something new—this individuality in its full flower—is a quite different way of the soul experiencing itself and the universe around it.

How, then, are you to understand the experience of will at the fourth level? Recall the idea of Ouspensky, presented in Chapter 2: Real Will is like suddenly seeing the solution to a mathematics problem. No doubt, we have all had the experience of working intently on some abstract issue which we knew had an answer but it seemed to elude us. Then, there may have come that instant in which we suddenly recognized the solution. The *feeling* of Real Will is much like that feeling associated with finding an answer which works.

This analogy is an especially effective one because it reminds us that the universe is orderly. The mathematician trusts that the array of scattered observations can be combined into some formula because he or she knows the universe is lawful. In the same way, we struggle with the scattered challenges and difficulties of our lives. Real Will is the recognition of creative possibilities for responding to those problems.

The Real Will or transpersonal will is that which reveals solutions. It does so by uniting the influences of life in order to create something new. The content of revelation from your transpersonal will is usually a surprise to you; its solution comes as something not considered by your personality-self. Often it is even rejected at first by your personality because of its unexpected or foreign quality. But it is this feature of "new possibilities" offered by Real Will which gives it a power to transform you far beyond the influences of Stage 3 will. *The answers and solutions proposed by empowering will are usually an extension of the personality we already are; transpersonal will reveals to us the invitation to be something more.*

We might well ask, "Why not go *directly* to Stage 4 will?" In other words, why don't we begin our efforts to awaken the will by merely inviting God's will to work through us? In fact, we can: but only because it is possible to work on developing slowly all four stages simultaneously. However, this does not mean we can bypass the first three stages. Before we concern ourselves with ultimate surrender, let us be sure that we have something of substance that we are offering up. Jung worked with his patients to develop a strong sense of individual nature (ego) before moving in the individuation process to transpersonal development. Assagioli's system teaches personal psychosynthesis before spiritual psychosynthesis. The Cayce readings encourage us to use fully at a personal level all we have at hand before expecting a higher power to gracefully intervene.

The development of the first three stages is crucial because those levels of will allow us to function in the physical plane. When we have moments in which transpersonal will awakens, the accompanying revelation will always require an application. The Real Will reveals solutions, but then the solutions must be lived in three-dimensional expression. If we have not worked to develop negating will and skillful will, as well as empowering will, then the insights, solutions, and possibilities uncovered by transpersonal will shall not truly benefit us. It is an irony of the spiritual path. We must work hard to achieve something and then be prepared to surrender it. Many times it will be given back to us, but always we must be ready to surrender it again.

Only by letting go and surrendering can you experience the highest level of will. But in what specific ways might you expect to encounter it? To what degree might you have already had small tastes of how it works?

The greatest example of surrender and transpersonal will is something you probably aren't ready for. It is Jesus' willingness to give up His personal powers and His personal desires. The scene in the Garden of Gethsemane is a lesson about letting go and being willing to follow God's plan. But even though you may not be ready for that kind of surrender, in smaller ways you have seen how it works.

Remember a day when you wanted things to go a certain way and worked hard to make it happen. Maybe it was a family reunion at your home, an important job interview, or a special vacation trip. There may have come a point where you knew that you had done all you could possibly do and now it was time just to let go. With that surrender there may have come a feeling of peace, and then some unexpected things happened. You may have seen events work out much better than you could ever have made them happen.

Or, you may have had this sort of experience with transpersonal will: a healing breakthrough in a difficult interpersonal relationship. You may have thought long and hard about how to act with this difficult person. You probably tried everything you knew how to do. Perhaps there were some improvements, but a real change seemed beyond your ability. But knowing you had done your best, you let go—you turned the problem over to something Higher. And then—like grace—it happened. Maybe you woke up one morning *knowing* what was needed. You hadn't arrived at this solution by logic. It was a gift; it was now a Higher Will directing you.

Summary and Examples of the Stages

Stages 0 through 4 are summarized in the chart on page 84. As you can note, the healthy/unhealthy polarity has meaning only for Stages 1 through 3. The essential features

to foster further developing are relevant to all stages except
the highest.

Stage #	Label	Polarity	Key features to facilitate development
4	Trans-personal		
3	Empowering	Wizard alchemist/ egomaniac manipulator	Humility, goodness, willingness to surrender
2	Skillful	Synergistic balancer/ compromiser who violates integrity	Understanding paradoxical nature of life
1	Negating	Affirmer of individuality/ negating, doubting cynic	Trust in life, hope, optimism
0	"Sleep"		Personal drive, such as pride or ambition

Let's see now how all five stages can be observed in a
single area of life. Three such examples are presented
below: the spiritual exercise of meditation, the process of
healing, and the attempt to change a habit pattern.

Meditation. Stage 4 will and all the other stages of will
development are depicted in meditation. This spiritual
discipline is a training exercise for the will. Imagine the
following steps you might go through in order to have a
deep meditation experience.

When you first sit down to meditate, your will is
probably still at Stage 0. When you close your eyes, the
tendency is for your mind to flit from one thought to
another. You are caught up in the worries and frustrations

of the day. But through an act of will you begin to focus your attention. You use Stage 1 will to say "no" to those distracting thoughts and you make the effort to keep all of your attention on the mantra or affirmation of your choice. The use of this type of will is effective, up to a point. It can move you to a deep level of concentration, but far more is required if you are to meditate effectively.

Awakening the second stage of the will, you can begin using any forthcoming distractions to take you actually deeper into the spirit of the affirmation. Employing skillful will, you can blend the content of the distraction with the motivation or ideal of the affirmation. For example, suppose that your affirmation is, "Let me be a channel of blessing to others." When a distracting thought arises about your father-in-law, there is an option other than using the negating will to force the distraction aside. Instead, you can use the thought of this person to remind you of a place in your life where the ideal of loving service could be applied. You might even take a moment to feel the channeling of blessings to your father-in-law. In so doing, you may experience deeper attunement.

Continuing this process, you come to a point in meditation where your mind begins to get still. Instead of the recurring parade of images and memories surfacing from your unconscious, there is stillness. Your mind has become the servant of your will. Will at the third stage has emerged. In this personally empowering state, much is possible in meditation. You feel re-energized and at the same time profoundly relaxed and at peace. However, this is the danger zone of meditation. In her classic book on meditative and mystical states entitled *Mysticism*, Evelyn Underhill describes this state of meditation as "The Quiet." She says that it tempts the meditator to believe that he or she has now arrived. The sense of personal expansiveness and personal empowerment is dangerous if you forget that there is yet a further step: one that requires a letting go.

The highest state of meditation is one in which the Real Will takes over. Here there can be a revelation of the purposes and insights of the soul. Ultimately meditation is surrender. In the end you can do nothing to *make* something happen, even with the considerable powers of Stage 3 will. There must come the surrender and the trust which allows a rebirth of your sense of identity.

Healing. The process of healing also demonstrates the developmental stages of will, particularly if healing is considered at the deepest levels of the soul and not alone the treatment of physical symptoms. As helpful a role as meditation, massage or surgery may play, real healing must include a change in consciousness—otherwise new symptoms are likely to emerge in the future.

When you are sick, you are to some extent "asleep" in old, familiar patterns which control your thinking, feeling, acting, and even body functioning. Whether the situation is chronic headaches or cancer, there is an aspect of the will that is at Stage 0 when illness occurs. Of course, a person sick with headaches, cancer or any other illness may have a strong, well-functioning will in some (even many) areas of life. However, the aspects of living which have produced the illness are controlled by forces which are not being directed by the will. Illness is "sleep"; dis-ease is unconsciousness (even though you may be painfully conscious of the symptoms).

Healing *begins* with a Stage 1 awakening of will in those areas which have been producing an imbalanced condition. It starts with being able to say "no." Negation could take the form of saying "no" to a self-image of being victimized by the illness. Or, it could be rejection of one's self-image as the sickly one. In other cases, Stage 1 will is necessary in order to start saying "no" to certain thought patterns, behavior or dietary habits which have maintained the illness.

However, healing must go deeper. Next, you are challenged to awaken Stage 2 will in these areas of life. This may mean skillfully balancing the inner and outer demands of life to making healing possible. It may mean embracing the illness itself and listening to it. Only when you reach Stage 2 will can you actually accept an illness and let it be your teacher. The symptoms of pain can often be a message—to the conscious mind or the soul itself—and the removal of symptoms may come only after the lesson has been appreciated and skillfully integrated into living.

With Stage 3 will it becomes possible for you actually to build a new body. As mind obeys the guiding direction of will and initiates new patterns of thought and emotion, then a new way of body functioning emerges. For example, biofeedback research has shown that with the will you can control and reprogram processes previously thought to be under the exclusive domain of the unconscious mind and automatic nervous system (e.g., blood pressure, skin temperature, heart rate). But even biofeedback (i.e., "the voluntary control of internal states," as it is often called) has its limitation. The willful removal of certain painful conditions may not amount to a real healing if the deeper cause of the illness is not dealt with. Stage 3 will may permit you to replace disfunctioning or sick aspects of your body with healthy ones, but if a healing in consciousness has not occurred, then different painful symptoms are likely to emerge.

Transpersonal will is required for the deepest level of the healing of any disease or illness. There is always an element of inexplicable grace to real healing. The progress that can be made in the healing *process* is, no doubt, important. The "will to health" unfolds as you move through Stages 1, 2 and 3. However, at some point you must be able to surrender and experience the Real Will of your individuality. It knows the deepest solution to your sickness. At Stage 4 you can find in its fullness the role of will in healing.

Changing habit patterns. Another practical example of the progressive stages of will development comes whenever you try to change some troublesome habit in your personality. To illustrate this, consider the example of Terry, a single, 29-year-old office manager. She has the bothersome habit of quickly losing her temper in a wide variety of interpersonal relations—at the job, with family or friends, with herself, etc. Whenever her mechanical, automatic habit of temper flare-ups is controlling her, then she is at Stage 0 will in this part of her life.

The first stage in healing this tendency is for her to learn that she can say "no" to the compulsion to blow her stack. As she slowly begins to experience that she has an identity other than the "hot-head," then she is making constructive progress, using her will to change this habit. However, to stop with Stage 1 would mean to settle for repression of her anger, a situation which cannot have long-term benefits. Simply repressed for an indefinite period, that anger would begin to pop up elsewhere in her life, most likely as physical illness.

To progress on to Stage 2, Terry can use her will to deal with her anger more skillfully. She might do it in at least two ways. First, she can re-embrace her anger and love it. She can recognize that there is something good in her anger, even if its way of expression hasn't been very constructive. Rather than seeing her anger as an irredeemable fault, she may start seeing its good side and skillfully find new ways of using its energy and determination. Second, her Stage 2 will can allow her to start seeing in a new way the people who make her angry. This level of will may allow Terry to perceive the faults and shortcomings of others in such a fashion that she recognizes the seed or essence of something good, even in the things that used to make her explode.

The changing of this pattern can proceed further under the direction of Stage 3 will. Now Terry can use her will to start building new patterns of thought and feeling toward those who used to make her automatically so angry. Here she is not merely finding different ways to *cope* with or *channel* anger—she is directing her mind with her will to create new attitudes and feelings.

The temptation is to see this third stage of will awakening as the final development Terry can make in changing this habit. By mastering Stage 3 will, she experiences a great sense of empowerment and knows that she can create whatever kinds of attitudes and feelings she wants to have toward people. Yet a more complete transformation of her problem is possible. If she listens for the promptings of Stage 4 will, she can discover a profoundly wise source of guidance, which can direct the shaping of the very *best* ways of seeing and responding to people in her life. This transpersonal will can provide the *optimal solution* to every interpersonal challenge she will face, often guiding her responses in ways that never would have occurred to her personality.

This illustration, as well as the previous ones concerning healing and meditation, are meant only as examples. There are many other situations in which you can experience this kind of sequential awakening of your will. No doubt you are at different stages with different relationships and issues. The first key for each area is to recognize the level of will development at which you currently live. Progress begins at that point. Once you recognize your current developmental level with a particular problem, then what can you do to move ahead?

The second key answers that question. Remember that most often you *cannot force* the progression. Even though you might want to set a goal to be at Stage 4 with a particular problem by next week, don't do it. Any kind of impatience only makes it more likely you shall revert to a lower stage of will in that area of life.

Because of your unique background as a soul, there is a specialized timing to how quickly you can proceed with will development in each challenging circumstance. In one relationship you may be able to make rapid progress; in another, it may take months or years to gain mastery of the next stage. But no matter what the timing, you can maintain a patient, persistent effort to remain at the healthy side of the will at whatever stage you find yourself.

RECOMMENDED ADDITIONAL READING

The Act of Will, Roberto Assagioli (Penguin Books, Baltimore, 1973)

The chapters in Part One of this book are especially relevant. Although Assagioli does not propose a strict developmental sequence, he writes at length about skillful will and transpersonal will.

In Search of the Miraculous, P.D. Ouspensky (Harcourt, Brace and Javonovich, New York, 1949)

Although the entire book is recommended reading, Chapter 8 especially deals with personality and essence.

Will and Spirit: A Contemplative Psychology, Gerald May (Harper and Row, San Francisco, 1982)

This lengthy book does not always stay on the topic of will, but there are very important sections dealing with the differences between "willfulness" and "willingness."

"How Do We Determine the Will of God," Herbert Weiner and Richard Drummond in *Venture Inward* (November/December, 1984), Volume 1, Number 2 (A.R.E. Press, Virginia Beach, Va.)

The article is a transcript of a thoughtful dialogue between a rabbi and a seminary professor. This ancient question is not easily answered but these two scholars provide some useful points.

PART TWO

Training and Using Your Will

CHAPTER FIVE

Techniques for Awakening the Will

Is it possible to train and develop your will? Some people say that the very phrase "will training" is circular reasoning. They point out that to awaken and develop the will by conscious effort is impossible, since the very activity presupposes that the will is already awake and able to direct the effort. This argument suggests that will training is like trying to "pull yourself up by your own boot straps" because it asks an undeveloped will to supervise its own training.

Such a pessimistic viewpoint is not a new one. It has been offered whenever human growth and development is proposed. Can people teach themselves—that is, can ignorance move toward understanding, or does learning always require a teacher who already knows? Can the unenlightened mind do anything on its own to move toward spiritual awakening, or does enlightenment always require a guru?

This sort of philosophical question is not easily answered, but a case shall be presented in this chapter demonstrating that there *are* things you can do which may further awaken and strengthen your will, in addition to keeping its function healthy. This chapter consists of twelve training exercises which may help you gain a conscious, balanced relationship with your will. Undoubtedly some of the exercises may seem more pertinent to you than others, and some may give you better results when applied. Approach this program as if it were a menu from which you can select and experiment.

Each one of these training strategies requires that some measure of will already be present in order to work with it.

If you are "asleep," then it may never occur to you to focus attention on one of the exercises. However, in a moment in which your will is at least awakened to Stage 1, you can focus attention and effort sufficiently to try an exercise.

Experience shows that you *do* have these momentary, almost spontaneous awakenings of will. They most likely occur at some of the times in the day when you face a choice. They may happen when you desire to make something different about your life and you remember that it is within your power to make those changes. Or, the small awakenings of conscious will may occur in an inexplicable fashion, as if there is deep within your unconscious life of the soul a faculty that in its own timing and way *can* awaken. But, by whatever means they occur, these moments are special opportunities. They provide you with a chance to direct attention and effort toward avenues which make possible a more healthy expression of will.

Training Exercise #1: Meditation

Many traditions of spiritual development recommend meditation both as a way to achieve higher states of mind as well as to strengthen and develop the will. The Cayce readings, for example, describe meditation as an exercise which partakes of the individuality and its accompanying characteristic of will.

In Chapter 4 we examined a way of viewing meditation in which it progressively engages higher and higher stages of the will. But you may still wonder, "What is a simple and direct way in which I can get started meditating?"

Perhaps the simplest starting point is a meditative technique which focuses attention on your breathing. Practice even for just five minutes a day the following exercise:

> Sit comfortably in a chair which keeps your back reasonably erect. Pick a setting which is likely to be quiet so that your attention won't be distracted by outside disturbances. With your eyes closed, move your attention gently to your breathing. You need not try to control the rate or the depth of your breathing, but simply keep your attention on the flowing in and out of each breathing cycle.

Practice this technique, and you shall quickly see how it demands the conscious presence of will. How easily attention becomes undirected and is captured by distractions. You may find it helpful to count breaths silently as an aid to keeping your focus. Or you may prefer to hold the attitude described by Lama Anagarika Govinda in his book *Creative Meditation and Multi-Dimensional Experience:*

> Thus we experience the very nature of life by surrendering ourselves to [breathing's] rhythm, instead of interfering with it, because it is the rhythm of the universe that breathes through us. Instead of thinking ourselves as the agents and originators of this movement ("*I* am breathing in; *I* am breathing out," etc.), we should rather feel "the universe breathes in me, streams through me; it is not *I* who is breathing, but the universe through me." (p. 119)

Of course, meditation can and should be viewed as something more profound than just sitting for five minutes and observing the breath. As a next step, use your will to keep attention on your highest spiritual aspiration. A mantra or affirmation is a good way to keep focused. It provides a centering point for the will. Nevertheless, attention upon the breath is in its own right a powerful will-training exercise and potentially a doorway to deep inner experiences.

Training Exercise #2: Small Group Work

Many great spiritual teachers, including Jesus and the Buddha, have worked with a small group. It is a potent vehicle for the seeker to change and grow spiritually. More specifically, there is something about a like-minded small group which facilitates the personal awakening of will. There is a special quality found within a group if it has a common ideal of spiritual development. The Cayce readings recognize this point and recommend a small group program for soul growth, centered around a curriculum of material called "A Search for God." Gurdjieff (as well as his protégés like Ouspensky and Nicoll) understood the power of a small group and often conducted his work in such a setting. The last fifteen years of Gurdjieff's life were spent in international travel, which included setting up groups to work with his system. In a parallel fashion, Steiner delivered a large portion of his teachings to small groups of his followers in various European cities.

What is it, then, about a small group that makes it such a special format? One possibility is that the group begins to forge a kind of "group consciousness." It acts like a field in which the personal unfoldment of each individual happens best. That field includes the features of a collective will or "pooled" will, from which each individual is able to draw in order to make choices and changes which might otherwise be much harder to accomplish alone.

The purpose is not to make the individual seeker dependent on the group. The "pooled" will is not meant to be more powerful than the individual's own awakening will, but rather a servant and helper to each individual. This is a critical distinction because groups *can* tragically turn into cults. The key rests with the *purpose* of the group. If its mission is to help each individual to flower in his or her own unique way, then a small group can be a powerful assistance for awakening and balancing the will. If the group honors the essential freedom of choice of each member, then it can be a safe method to enhance will development.

Keeping the guidelines in mind, you may want to experiment with this approach. Try a regular group activity which works with some system for spiritual growth. The system may or may not directly involve a discussion of the will itself, but it should be one which stresses personal application and responsibility. Every group is different because of the unique chemistry created by the participants. But if you can find a group which feels right to you, it may be one of the very best strategies for strengthening your will.

Training Exercise #3: Self-Observation

Learn to "stand aside and watch yourself go by." As an exercise in will, step outside yourself and observe your own thoughts, emotions, and deeds. The goal is an objective point of view. In other words, the point of this technique is *not* to be narcissistic or preoccupied with yourself. Instead, this exercise requires you to use your will to disengage your full identity momentarily from the strong habits which usually control your thinking, feeling, and acting.

In using this technique, you do not stop your inner and outer reactions to life, but instead merely observe them in an objective way. One part of you continues without re-sistence in habit patterns, while another part of you disengages or disidentifies long enough to observe the habit *as it is happening.* Only through exercising your will can such a technique be accomplished.

To illustrate how the technique might work, suppose that you have made a hurried stop-over at the bank during your lunch hour. Standing in line waiting for a teller is taking far longer than expected and you are going to be late getting back to the office. All kinds of automatic, habitual reactions arise quite predictably. They come from the part of you which has no free will and operates like a machine. Frustration, anger, worry, a churning stomach, restlessly moving around in line—all these may occur. If there is any hope for your will to alter some day those old, familiar reactions, it won't be through repression of them. Instead, it can start from the simple yet subtle technique of "standing aside and watching yourself go by." *While* these reactions are taking place, you can use your will to move in con-sciousness so that you are able to observe objectively what is happening.

The quality of this self-observation *must* be loving acceptance. It serves no useful purpose to condemn yourself or to feel guilty. But as you learn to use your will to withdraw some of your energy and identity from those automatic habits, a surprising thing occurs. It may take weeks or months of self-observation (maybe longer), but the controlling force of that habit begins to weaken. In what may have seemed like a roundabout method, your will has been used to make a change. Instead of trying to use the will to force that change, this more gentle technique produces better results.

This powerful method of self-observation is not reserved for only negative emotional states. Nearly everyone spends most of daily living in a kind of sleeping wakefulness. The most innocuous and unemotional routines of life are good candidates for self-observation. As your will becomes stronger and more fully awakened, you shall find it easier to sustain these periods of objective self-perception. What initially could be done for only seconds at a time may be maintained for several minutes. The fruits of this technique can also include important insights about yourself which give you material for the next technique.

Training Exercise #4:
Disciplines Countering Your Habits

Habit is the very antithesis of authentic will. Whenever you use your will to make efforts against the grain of the familiar, then the health and strength of your will can be enhanced. Carefully selected personal disciplines or consciousness experiments are one way to do this. Here are some examples.

Speak about other people only in the way you would if they were present to hear what you'd say about them.

Smile at strangers whom you pass.

At mealtimes eat *all* of one item on your plate before moving on to the next.

Underplan your day—i.e., leave time and room for surprises or the unexpected.

Use your opposite hand more often—i.e., if you are righthanded, use your left hand more often than usual.

Go without saying "I" for a day.

There is, of course, a degree of artificiality to any such discipline. However, these examples are not necessarily meant to become permanent features of your behavior. For instance, whereas it may be a productive will-training exercise for a righthander to use her left hand more frequently for a day or two, it is not expected that she would try to incorporate this "going against the grain of habit" indefinitely. In a similar fashion, it is probably impractical to eliminate permanently saying "I", but it can be a valuable exercise for 24 hours. On the other hand, smiling more often or speaking of others with more sensitivity may be will-training exercises worth incorporating as often as the discipline can be remembered.

To use this technique, you must first have observed yourself. You need to have recognized some of your strongest habits which occur in a mechanical, will-less way. Then you can decide upon appropriate experiments for using will—small exercises which introduce a conscious new approach. Some of your disciplines are likely to challenge you to more loving or thoughtful behavior (e.g., smiling at strangers), although other disciplines can be value neutral and merely challenge you to bring more consciousness to what you do (e.g., changing your style of eating from your dinner plate).

Another version of this training strategy is to do something you dislike or "isn't like you." Of course, you should always make sure that any such disciplne doesn't require you to operate against your highest ideals. However, with that important criterion in mind, consider these two examples.

When you need to ask a favor of an out-of-town friend, which method is more natural to your habitual personality—write a letter or telephone? As an act of will, you might try to do the one that "goes against the grain" of your tendency.

When you sit next to someone on a bus or airplane, what seems more natural for you to do—keep quiet unless spoken to or initiate conversation? Again, a will-training exercise for you might be to consciously try out the behavior that "isn't like you."

Training Exercise #5: Loving Self-Assertion

Much has been made of self-assertion techniques in popular psychology. Interest has largely focused on training women in the skills of assertion, but the topic is relevant to male psychology as well. The question remains whether or not such training is conducive to spiritual growth, and more specifically what relationship it has to the expression of a healthy will.

Students of the Cayce readings have been surprised to find instances in which self-assertiveness is directly recommended to individuals as a prescription for their spiritual development. For example one man was told:

> The entity because of his indecisions at times allows others to take advantage of him. The entity must learn to be self-assertive; not egotistical but self-assertive—from a knowledge of the relationship of self with the material world . . .
>
> Then, know thyself first. Know thine own abilities. Don't assert that you know something and don't . . . Don't allow others to talk you out of decisions you have reached.   3018-1

If the meaning of the phrase "self-assertion" is first made clear, then practicing self-assertion can be a positive step toward a healthy will. When the "self" in question refers to your essential, inner being—your individuality—then healthy will training is possible. But if the "self" refers to the old, habitual, fear-based patterns of personality, then assertion only undermines your real will by putting you further "asleep."

In a similar way, it is helpful to clarify the word "assertion." It can have connotations of aggressiveness, and this hardly leads to a healthy will. Instead, it is possible to understand assertion in terms of *affirmation*. It means the practical expression of your will to say clearly to the world around you, "This is who I am."

There are many helpful ways to practice this kind of creative self-assertion. One is to express positive feelings. As an act of will, practice communicating good feelings. Use your will first to put aside fears that you are being corny, pushy or prideful. Then, when it is appropriate and honest, use your will and affirm words like these:

> I really enjoy being with you.
> I feel good about what I just accomplished.
> Thanks for appreciating me.
> I really like the way you handled that.

Another kind of self-assertion skill is to set limits. In many ways this incorporates a balanced use of Stage 1 will because it requires that you say "no" to certain things. By communicating to others the parameters in which you are willing to relate to them, you affirm who you are. Of course, the examples below may not fit the limits you want to set. But as you express your *own* limits by loving self-assertion, you are using and strengthening your will. For example:

Thanks, but I don't need any help.
I wish that you wouldn't make commitments for me.
I would appreciate your not smoking.
I would like to think further about that before deciding what to do.

Training Exercise #6: Stay in the Now

To train and strengthen your will, keep your attention in the now. Act in the now. It sounds simple, but most people have great difficulty doing this. Consider some of the ways in which you may try to use your will out of sync with its natural, effective place: in the present moment.

(a) Do you fantasize and rehearse well in advance what you are going to do and say? Do you constantly anticipate the future, dwelling on scenarios that may or may not even happen? This mistaken use of the will goes far beyond prudent thoughts or plans about the future; it exhausts your will. When you carefully observe your thought patterns, do you find anxiety-directed visualizations about the future (e.g., a showdown with the boss or a date with an idolized member of the opposite sex)? There is a great problem created by such attempts to force the future along a certain course. It is not only a waste of mental energy, but the event never turns out as anticipated. When you confront the situation as it finally manifests, it is different than expected and suddenly your will is disoriented and ineffective.

(b) How often do you catch yourself trying to use your will to *force* something to happen "before its time has come"?

This phrase may sound poetic, but nature itself shows the deep wisdom in "right timing." Living organisms, like the human psyche and body, are largely governed by hidden rhythms and destinies.

Here a misuse of the will is to impose a conscious agenda on some developing process. In what ways might you find yourself doing this? Perhaps in trying to get a friend interested in transpersonal theories before he or she has a firm grounding in a healthy ego strength. Or, attempting to get your garden to produce ripe tomatoes a week earlier than normal. As a parent, do you push your preschool child to grow up too soon, learning to read or do arithmetic before other children? Or trying to lose 10 pounds when your body isn't ready for the discipline that may be required. The possibilities are endless, and only by careful self-observation can you see how you may be misapplying your will to force things out of their natural timing.

(c) Do you try to change your past? This erroneous use of will goes beyond a healthy consideration of the lessons to be learned from past experiences. Most frequently, this misapplication of will involves continually dwelling on some mistake, as if you could change what happened merely by willing it to be so. However, your capacity to make changes resides in the present moment alone. Only in the now is your will able to express its potent capabilities to direct and alter the course of life.

In a sense this particular will-training exercise is the most fundamental one. Other techniques, such as meditation, self-observation and self-assertion, all require your attention and point of application to be in the present moment.

Training Exercise #7: Positive Imitation

The next four training exercises are adapted from the teachings of Rudolf Steiner, specifically regarding the education of the will in children. The Waldorf School curriculum, founded on Steiner's philosophy, includes many principles concerning the awakening of a healthy will function. Although each of these four training strategies are most fundamentally relevant to work with children, we can infer that to some degree they can be adapted and made applicable to adult efforts to awaken and educate the will.*

The first of the four techniques is *positive imitation.* Your will can be awakened and strengthened by observing other people who have a healthy will. You can learn by their example how to use your own will. In the Waldorf School setting, the example is the teacher, but as adults you must identify your "teachers" in a more informal way.

To get this started, review the seven qualities of the will outlined in Chapter 3. Who *are* the people in your life who do a better job than you in manifesting those qualities? Can you find more time to be with such people? Or can you at least be more attentive when you are around them as to *how* they deal with the challenges of life? These attentive efforts can show results as you learn to demonstrate your own healthy will through purposeful imitation.

Another, and more indirect, method to work with this training approach is to read and study biographical accounts of great men and women who manifested a healthy will. Some readers find that the objective, narrative approach of a biographer is most helpful in learning about the will. Others find that the subjective, personal account provided by an autobiography is more meaningful, because it provides a more direct way to experience the thinking, feeling, and willing processes of that great person.

Training Exercise #8: Building Rhythms into Life

In the Waldorf School setting, the will is educated in the context of meaningful repetition and rhythm. The child is taught the natural rhythms of living—those organic patterns found in the earth's seasons, the cycles of plant growth, and even the recurrent elements in the cycle of a single day. As adults, there is much that can still be learned

---

*For insights into Steiner's approach to educating the will and these four training approaches, the author is indebted to Robert Witt, Waldorf School teacher and administrator.

by the appreciation of purposeful, conscious repetitions in life.

The will is awakened and trained through repetition in more than one way. First, there must be willed effort to maintain the pattern. Once the pattern is established, the will can, in turn, begin to draw sustenance from the rhythm itself.

This process is illustrated in the discipline of keeping a regular meditation time each day. At first it takes effort. All kinds of excuses to procrastinate or avoid keeping the appointed time arise from the mind. By acts of will the regular pattern is established. However, with the creation of such a personal rhythm, a remarkable thing begins to happen. The rhythm has a life of its own. Keeping the meditation time becomes easier, no longer requiring a struggle or undue effort. The will itself begins to be fed and strengthened by the purposeful pattern.

Consider how you might use this training exercise in your own life. First, are there ways that you could start being sensitive to the rhythms of nature? Your will can be nurtured as you consciously participate in those patterns. Perhaps it means paying attention to sunrises and sunsets. Or it might be an involvement in the seasons of nature through a backyard vegetable garden or a fruits and berries orchard.

Second, select one or two personal behaviors that can be established as personal rhythms. It may be meditation, reading, exercise, playtime with children, or any other purposeful activity that can be repeated regularly.

Training Exercise #9: Let Go of Mechanization

Society offers an incredible array of labor-saving machines. There are so many shortcuts to getting things done which are available to members of Western technological culture. The list seems endless. Each device saves you time and most significantly it saves you *effort*.

But what price do you pay for becoming more and more dependent upon machines and appliances to avoid effort? Aren't there both overt and subtle ways in which your will is undermined? A labor-saving device permits your force of will to remain inactive or even asleep. For example, excessive use of movies and television for entertainment destroys your own capacity for will-directed imagination. Why should the will be alive and playfully active with the mind, when it is possible to sit back passively and receive fascinating images?

But if you are serious about awakening and training your will, just how far should you take this? Surely it is not practical or necessary to return to life styles of the 18th century just to have a healthy will. Surely spiritual growth is not made more efficient by throwing out vacuum cleaners, electric toothbrushes, and power drills. Most likely your present way of living and your commitments do not make it possible to eliminate many labor-saving machines. But rather than just to ignore the impact they have on your will, it is still possible to design some will-enhancing *experiments* which reintroduce personal effort to areas where avoidance with a machine is easy.

For example, suppose you enjoy music in your life. Perhaps you are the sort of person who can play one or more instruments in a marginally skillful and amateurish way. Rather than flip on the stereo or radio every time you want some music, you could periodically use your will to create your own music. Certainly it won't be of the professional calibre that you would hear otherwise, but you are likely to discover a vast *qualitative* difference in your experience of music when your will is involved.

Or, consider the short trips which you make by automobile, which could have been accomplished by walking or biking. It may take some planning because of the longer time involved, but it can reawaken you to the meaning of physical distance (something easily lost by the hypnotic effect of modern auto and jet travel).

If you are a public speaker, occasionally try to make your presentation without an amplification system. Obviously there are settings which make this impossible. In some auditoriums it would mean that many people just wouldn't hear your unaided voice. But aren't there times when you use electronic amplification out of habit or because you won't have to make as concerted an effort to reach people with your voice? What you are likely to discover is that your voice, directly received by listeners without the intervention of a mechanical device, creates a different kind of relationship between you and your audience. At least in part, this is the product of your will as a more active force in the relationship.

Structure your experimental disciplines as you did in Training Exercise #4 (i.e., "Disciplines Countering Your Habits"). Your efforts to do something without a labor-saving machine may be for only a short period of time. For example, use a manual instead of electric can opener for a week. Or your experiment may take the form of a regular commitment. For example, once each week replace one short automobile trip with a walk; or write one letter a week when you would usually have made a long-distance phone call instead.

It is not the purpose of this training exercise to alienate you from the modern world. No doubt, effort-saving machines shall continue to be a large part of your life. But taking them for granted and ignoring the indirect influence they have on will is inadvisable. Merely the *occasional* reliance upon your own efforts instead of a machine's can help keep your will alert. In so doing, your will is available to use creatively the time that the machines free up for you.

Training Exercise #10: Moving the Limbs of the Body Purposefully

In Steiner's system of thought, there are three key functions: thinking, feeling, and willing. In correlating these three with the parts of the physical body, the following associations are made:

Thinking especially engages the head and brain;

Feeling especially engages the trunk and internal organs;

Willing especially engages the limbs.

In the Waldorf Schools, the child is given will-educating activities which purposefully involve movement of the arms and legs. Because the associations described above continue throughout human life, this training strategy is probably pertinent to adult will training as well.

As part of your personal program to awaken your will further, you may wish to select some kind of activity which involves purposeful body movements. For some people, will training is achieved through hatha yoga practice or T'ai Chi exercises. For others, it can happen through a regular program of running, walking or biking. For those who have access to skilled teachers of Gurdjieff's system, there is training in his elaborate "movements," which require an awakening of the will forces. In a similar fashion there are schools which offer instruction in Steiner's eurythmy, body movements which make visible the realms of music and voice.

In a sense this training exercise is the most straightforward of the twelve presented in this chapter. Depending on what approach you choose, varying amounts of dedication are required, but it is easy to see how bodily movement requires the use of will.

Training Exercise #11: Choose Your Spiritual Ideal

Your will puts into action your values and beliefs. It is the ingredient that implements the ideal you hold for your life. Not only is your will involved in *applying* your ideal, but it is a crucial factor in *setting* that ideal. Not only does the will implement your ideal, it also chooses it. The training exercise is something you do once, although later you may want to review your choice and decide whether or not a new spiritual ideal is more appropriate.

We will explore more deeply in Chapter 9 the qualities of a spiritual ideal. But now you can complete the simple but very important step of choosing your ideal. Ask yourself these two questions:

What human qualities do I value most (e.g., peace, love, honesty, etc.)?

In these moments when I am my "best self," in what direction do I want my life to go?

With your answers to these two questions in mind, you can now summarize your thoughts in a more succinct way. In a single word or a short phrase, write down your spiritual ideal. It is a description of the quality of living or state of consciousness to which you aspire. The spiritual ideal is not the particular goals or actions you hope to accomplish; instead, it describes the *spirit* in which you want to live—the sense of purpose and motivation you want to have. For example, here are wordings that different people have chosen for their ideal: compassion, patient service, creative loving.

What you choose as an ideal is a major spiritual goal. Most likely you have only occasional days when you are able to live that way. You may take years or even a lifetime making personal efforts to grow toward that ideal. For this reason it's important to start applying Training Exercise #12 right after you have chosen your spiritual ideal.

Training Exercise #12:
Set a Reachable Goal Daily

As the adage says, "Nothing succeeds like success." Nothing gives you a clearer, stronger sense of your will than to use it successfully. But a major obstacle you may face in training your will is the temptation to force the accomplishment of ideals too quickly—to try to change something with your will which for the moment is really beyond your reach.

Imagine a high jumper who wishes she could clear a height of six feet. She knows from experience that she can regularly clear five feet, but the six-foot level seems far beyond her current abilities—only a wish, a dream. But she is determined to make this change in her abilities. She intends to use her will and to accomplish her goal.

How then should she proceed? One option is for her to set the high jump bar at six feet every day in her practice sessions and continually try to clear it. She is going to have continual failures, but she hopes that eventually she might succeed.

Another option is to set little goals that progressively move her toward her ultimate goal. First, she would set the high jump bar at five feet one inch. She would work to clear that height consistently and, in so doing, build up her feeling of success and confidence. Inch by inch she would work her way up. Each new goal would be a small step, requiring her will to call forth just a little more strength and skill. These small, reachable goals would provide her with feelings of confidence and success, which are likely to lead to her larger goal.

The analogy is pertinent to your own life. Create for yourself the daily experience of successfully using your will. Each night before you go to bed or first thing in the morning, set a reachable goal. It is something that requires a little effort—a reasonable application of your will—but it is certainly within your capability to do it. Probably the goal is going to be something new each day, but some of them may be repeated. They may lead progressively toward a more ambitious goal, or they may be diverse and each day address something different in your life. Here are some examples, although you should make up your own list:

Compliment my wife once.

Do five minutes of calisthenics before breakfast.

Read five pages in the book I've been trying to get through.

Write one letter to a friend.

Smile at one stranger I pass on the sidewalk.

Remember, create just one reachable goal each day. Then, get it done. Experience a success with your will. Get to know that feeling of accomplishment. These small, daily successes build on each other and create for you greater confidence. They lead to a healthier, stronger will.

Summary

Design a will-training program for yourself, using as many of these twelve exercises as you like. They can be done in any order and you may be able to work on several of them during the same period of time. You are encouraged to design some kind of chart to keep track of your commitments and results with specific exercises. Use the sample chart which appears as Appendix A or create a more suitable one.

RECOMMENDED ADDITIONAL READING

The Inner Power of Silence, Mark Thurston (Inner Vision, Virginia Beach, Virginia, 1986)

The fundamentals of how to meditate are clearly explained in Chapter 3.

Creative Meditation and Multi-dimensional Consciousness, Lama Govinda (Theosophical Publishing House, Wheaton, Illinois, 1976)

An extraordinarily rich book of philosophy and practical techniques for meditation. Govinda repeatedly demonstrates his profound understanding of how Eastern and Western spirituality can meet. This orientation is fundamentally Buddhist, but as a man born in Germany and personally raised in a Western culture, he contributes a unique perspective of this most important spiritual discipline.

Psychological Commentaries on the Teachings of Gurdjieff and Ouspensky, Maurice Nicoll (Shambhala Press, Boulder, Colorado, 1984)

Nicoll is perhaps the only professional person who studied directly with Jung, Gurdjieff, and Ouspensky. He was for many years an authorized teacher of Ouspensky's system. This five-volume series contains edited transcripts of his classes during the 1940s in England. Of special note to will training are commentaries on self-observation and commentaries on going against habits.

Experiments in a Search for God and **Experiments in Practical Spirituality,** Mark Thurston (A.R.E. Press, Virginia Beach, Virginia, 1976 and 1980)

These two books each contain approximately 100 specific will-training exercises, many of which involve self-observation, going against a habit pattern, or initiating new responses to life. Each experiment includes a commentary explaining the rationale. The exercises are linked to chapters in the Cayce spiritual development growth sequence called "A Search for God."

Self-Assertion for Women, Pamela Butler (Harper and
 Row, New York, 1981)

This book is for women *and* men, although most of the
examples are drawn from the lives of women struggling to
better affirm their identity. It is a highly practical book that
shows you how to do it, even teaching with specific ways to
word your self-assertive responses. Dr. Butler repeatedly
demonstrates that self-assertion can best be done with
love—authentic self-love plus love and respect for others.
The examples in Training Exercise #5 of this chapter are
drawn from her work.

"The Magical Mysterious Human Will" by Robert Witt in
 Venture Inward, Volume 2, No. 1, January/February,
 1986.

CHAPTER SIX

Guidance, Decision Making and Will

When you face an important decision in your life, how do you proceed? How do you go about making a choice when you realize that the decision can have an important impact on your own life and the lives of others? Perhaps you are the sort of person who likes to go with the first, intuitive impression. Or maybe you favor a deliberate, analytical technique that carefully considers every variable. These are but two of many examples of decision-making style; however, every style makes use of the human will in some fashion.

Many people incorporate some type of guidance procedure in the course of making an important decision. The guidance may come from inner, subjective sources (e.g., dream guidance, meditation guidance) or outer sources (e.g., counseling, psychic readings, etc.). To seek guidance is to recognize one's own limited perspective on the decision at hand. It requires a degree of humility on the part of the conscious ego-self sincerely to receive help in making a choice.

To see the role that the will plays in guidance and decision making, let's first consider the three broad strategies that can be used. Each of the three represents a different response to this question: "What are you looking for when you seek guidance?"

1. Looking for an **answer.** This is the most obvious and probably the most frequent response. But it isn't *always* the best approach.

Using this strategy, you seek guidance which provides a

specific solution to a specific question. For example, you
might pose questions like these:

"Should I keep taking my medication despite its side
effects?"

"Should I finally tell my next-door neighbor what's been
irritating me about his behavior for the past six months?"

"What new type of vocation should I explore?"

In each of these instances, the exact *answer itself* is sought.

What sources of guidance might you want to pursue in
following this first approach? One effective method is to
get advice from a professional—perhaps a physician or a
counselor. Or, sometimes a trusted, knowledgeable friend
provides just as much helpful guidance. But you might
want to consider certain nontraditional methods as well—a
psychic, an astrologer, a numerologist, etc. Obviously,
your choice must be appropriate to your question. For
example, an astrologer may be more likely to give helpful
guidance on vocational choices than on medication side
effects.

To what extent can these esoteric methods of guidance be
relied upon? The philosophy in the Cayce readings
provides two useful guidelines. First, remember that your
life is not preordained. On a daily basis you are creating
your future through the choices you make, and no esoteric
art can define a predetermined future for you.

Second, esoteric arts are able to describe accurately
about 20% of the significant influences. That 20% may make
a significant impact on the problem at hand, but the
remaining 80% of the influence rests with how you use your
will. For example, astrology, numerology, and palmistry
might be able to describe accurately 20% of the influences
that should be taken into account when choosing a
vocation. But it would hardly seem wise to base the
decision entirely on this technique for receiving guidance.
In fact, these approaches probably serve us better when
they are part of the second strategy described below.

2. Looking for more **information.** This approach to guidance
is to search for additional information so you can formulate your *own* answer at a later time. With this technique,

you reserve the role of final decision making for your conscious will, but ask your unconscious self to give you more facts or additional perspectives which might lead to a better answer. Here are examples of questions which might lend themselves naturally to this approach:

"How should I respond to my boss? I don't know what he's feeling or why his actions are so confusing to me."

"What is best for my relationship with Richard? What kind of past-life experiences have we had which make me so attracted to him?"

In these two examples, the seeker is hoping to arrive eventually at a decision on how to act toward the boss or how deeply to get involved with Richard. Yet inner guidance is sought only to provide the information that might lead to a better conscious decision.

3. Looking for **confirmation.** This third approach seeks confirmation of a tentative conscious decision. In this instance the questioner looks for an inner sense of affirmation *or* warning concerning an intended course of action. For instance, one might pose these questions to the inner self:

"Will it be best for my daughter if I follow through on the decision to enroll her in a private school?"

"Is the best financial result to be expected from following through on the planned sales of my automotive stock?"

None of these three approaches is clearly superior to the other two for all situations, although some situations will be best suited to one of the three. In your own decision making, focus as often as possible on the second and third approaches. In other words, you should be careful about turning the *entire* decision-making process over to the unconscious or to someone else.

Here's another way to say this: God wants you to learn how to make decisions. In the Divine Plan for humanity, your personal will is to be awakened and used in a constructive manner. Yet, paradoxically, it is in your best interests spiritually to befriend and cooperate with an unconscious will that is always available to direct you wisely. The paradoxical nature of this principle can be frustrating. Yet you arrive at the best approach for attuned decision making when you find a balance between two kinds of will —(1) your conscious personal capacity to choose and (2) the deeper understanding of a Transpersonal Will within your unconscious.

The distinction between a conscious and an unconscious will has the potential to be the most significant breakthrough in psychology since a similar understanding emerged concerning the mind. Just think what an impact Freud and his contemporaries have had on modern culture by convincingly demonstrating the reality of the unconscious mind. That hidden side of the mind may have been dimly felt and usually dismissed, but Freud and others showed its powerful influence. The same qualities hold true of the unconscious will. We typically ignore its promptings and only dimly recognize its presence; and yet the unconscious will is potently active in our lives every day.

Modern science in its own rigorous, experimental way has found evidence that much of what we call conscious decision making is foreshadowed unconsciously in the brain just a moment before the decision reaches awareness. This may be suggestive of a broader and even more significant process in our unconscious life.

Dr. Leslie Farber, in his book *The Ways of Will*, proposes a theory which depicts the workings of two sides of the will—conscious and unconscious. Basing his ideas largely on observations from his psychiatric studies and practice, he calls the familiar, conscious will "Realm #2 will." It is characterized by the following qualities:

- is immediately experienced
- is goal oriented
- employs conscious efforts

In contrast he calls the unconscious will "Realm #1 will," which points to its more fundamental nature in the psyche. Its qualities include:

- usually recognized only in retrospect
- focuses on a process or way instead of a specific goal
- is generally effortless and linked to a "knowing" without necessarily having logical reasons

Since Realm #2 will is already familiar to his readers, Farber devotes more attention to examples of Realm #1 will. He assumes that the workings of the latter are a part of our experience, but we haven't known how to label these distinctive moments. He gives two especially clear examples which can be summarized in the following way.

1. When you examine your own biography, do you see situations in which you made a decision that, at the time, seemed rather trivial but in retrospect can be appreciated as momentous? With this retrospective view you may get the feeling that something unconscious within you knew the pathway down which that seemingly small decision would lead you. It may have been a decision to get in touch with an old friend, which unexpectedly led to a new job opportunity and a move to a new city. Or it may have been a casual decision to pick an unusual book off the library shelf which later led to a new philosophy of life and a different circle of friends.

2. "Knowing" for no logical reason that you just have to do something, although you cannot give any good explanation why. Or conversely, it may be that you just "know" you cannot do something that your conscious mind and will are ready to do. It may be knowing that you cannot marry someone even though all factors look favorable. Or it may be knowing that you must get in touch with someone, even though there is no reason to expect a productive result.

These "knowings" sound like "intuition." In fact, Rudolf Steiner describes the way in which the three human faculties—thinking, feeling, and willing—can be transformed into higher modes of knowing as they are directed by Spirit. Transformed willing he called Intuition.*

---

*Transformed thinking he called Imagination; and transformed feeling, Inspiration.

In addition to these two examples, it is helpful to note the priority which Realm #2 will gives to specific goals, accomplishments, and plans. In contrast, Realm #1 will tends to focus on a process or thematic way of approaching life. (This distinction is similar to one that will be made in Chapter 9 concerning your soul's mission.) Your soul's purpose in this incarnation—something to which Realm #1 will is especially sensitive, even though Realm #2 may not be—is fundamentally a theme, a *way* of approaching life. In other words, there is a kind of active willing within you which knows of the thematic way in which you can best contribute and grow for this lifetime. It operates rather unconsciously, but if its promptings are recognized, it still leaves much for the conscious Realm #2 will to do. Even if you begin to see the way or direction in which the deep unconscious will wants you to follow, many decisions still remain about *how* to accomplish it.

To get a further idea of the unconscious will and one of the ways it can operate, consider the following story. It is told in William James' long chapter on the human will, found in his classic book entitled *Principles of Psychology* (1890). In our modern times of central heating, it may be hard to appreciate fully the dilemma that James describes, but the reader is invited to imagine what it might be like to face this minor crisis of will on a cold, New England morning:

> We know what it is to get out of bed on a freezing morning in a room without a fire, and how the very vital principle within us protests against the ordeal. Probably most persons have lain on certain mornings for an hour at a time unable to brace themselves to the resolve. We think how late we shall be, how the duties of the day will suffer; we say, "I *must* get up, this is ignominious," and so on. But still the warm couch feels too delicious, and the cold outside too cruel, and resolution faints away and postpones itself again and again just as it seemed on the verge of the decisive act. Now how do we ever get up under such circumstances? If I may generalize from my own experience, we more often than not get up without any struggle or decision at all. We suddenly find that we *have*

got up. A fortunate lapse of consciousness occurs; we forget both the warmth and the cold; we *fall into some reverie connected with the day's life,* in the course of which the idea flashes across us, "Hello! I must lie here no longer"—an idea which at that lucky instant awakens no contradictory or paralyzing suggestions, and consequently produces immediately its appropriate motor effects. It was our acute consciousness of both the warmth and the cold during the period of struggle which paralyzed our activity... (Volume 2, p. 524)

Could this be an illustration of the influence produced by Realm #1 will? The crucial question concerns what goes on in the period James calls "a fortunate lapse of consciousness." That moment may best be interpreted not as having gone back to sleep, but instead as a brief time in which *Realm #2 will has given up.* Such a surrender creates a window of opportunity in which the Realm #1 will can present something to conscious awareness: a new sense of personal identity, the identity of one who is up and about the day's affairs. Now, getting up is easy and natural.

Recall from our definitions in Chapter 2 that the will is the faculty which shapes a sense of who we are. It directs attention to specific attitudes and feelings. Through a "fortunate lapse in consciousness" whereby the conscious will surrenders its fruitless efforts, the unconscious will is able to step in to provide just what is needed: a new sense of personal identity. That new identity has no problem getting up because its values are all invested in activities which lie outside of a warm bed.

You may have experienced a process in your own life similar to that recounted by James. Have you ever battled with yourself to do something, but the forced efforts of conscious will just weren't working? In such a situation have you finally given up or momentarily forgotten about the dilemma? If so, you may have discovered that when the problem comes back to your consciousness, you are now surprised to find that it is an easy, almost effortless, matter to do what is needed to be done. This is one of the ways in which Realm #1 will can subtly reveal its influence.

   Returning to Farber's theory, we find that this basic
model of two realms of will leads to a premise: The
beginning of healthy will development is the recognition of
the two *domains* of life which they govern. In other words,
Realm #1 will is especially capable of awakening certain
changes and qualities which are impossible for the
conscious efforts of Realm #2 will. In a similar fashion,
there are other qualities which can be accomplished only
through Realm #2 will. The following examples should
make this distinction clearer.

   A classic example of these two domains is particularly
familiar to insomniacs. Using Realm #2 will you can take a
hot bath, drink a glass of warm milk, and get comfortable in
bed. But you *cannot* use that realm of will to *make* yourself
go to sleep. Another kind of will which is outside normal
awareness makes that change in consciousness, and only in
retrospect (i.e., the next morning) do you observe that it
was successful. Farber extends the list of examples, as
shown in the chart below. The items in the left-hand column
can all be accomplished by a conscious effort of will. In fact,
those items cannot be produced by Realm #1 will. The
corresponding changes or human qualities listed in the
right-hand column seem to emerge from the unconscious
life with a will of their own. To varying degrees, doing the
things listed in the left-hand column may *aid* the awakening but it merely sets the stage and is not causative. For
example, getting comfortable in bed may be a prerequisite
to falling asleep but it doesn't cause sleep.

Domain of Realm #2 Will	Domain of Realm #1 Will
go to bed	fall asleep
obtain knowledge	show wisdom
act meekly	be humble
behave self-assertively	be courageous
offer congratulations	feel admiration
follow religious practices	have faith

   Farber proposes that the frequent mistake of a disordered will is to try to have the work of Realm #1 done by Realm #2 will. For example, we mistakenly think we can force or earn faith; or, we imagine that genuine courage is simply a matter of willing certain daredevil acts. But there are portions of our lives which do not yield to the force of conscious will and must, therefore, wait on a wise, unconscious will and its own sense of timing. Nowhere is this principle more important than in guidance and decision making.

Imagine, for example, that you face a dilemma. It's a problem that requires a choice and the application of that decision. If you follow the most frequent human tendency, you shall use your conscious mind to analyze the situation and arrive at a solution. Depending on your style, you may decide quickly or deliberately. You may consult others for their perspectives on the problem or you may rely on no one else. But no matter what style you follow, you shall probably arrive at a solution which conceives of the problem in terms of will and proposes specific things which you must do to change conditions or bring about desired results.

From one point of view, this all sounds quite admirable. It sounds like taking charge of your life—accepting responsibility and using the will to shape your own destiny. However, seen from another angle, it is incomplete. The natural human tendency to decision making does not appreciate that there may also be an unconscious realm of will, with its own wisdom, abilities at problem solving and timing.

So, in this hypothetical scenario, you arrive at a decision using only conscious elements. Your solution requires Realm #2 will to perform certain tasks, so designed that *the resolution to the dilemma depends solely upon their achievement.* But in so doing two critical activities are blocked. Two essential ways are masked in which the unconscious will could have been a co-creator with the conscious will to arrive at the *best* solution. Here are the two ways that are so often ignored:

1. The unconscious will can work on the *imaginative forces* of the mind to present new possibilities and potential answers. The word "imagination" in this case refers to a broad range of experiences and does not connote merely daydream fantasy.

For example, the imaginative forces express themselves in dreams, with the unconscious will acting as a choreographer of the mental thought forms which present the dream story. Not every dream is a guidance dream from God, but nearly every dream can teach us something. Even guidance dreams stimulated by Realm #1 will do not always present the "right" solution. They may instead offer the conscious self a new angle for seeing the old problem, or they may precognitively show what's ahead if the inclinations of Realm #2 will are followed.

The imaginative forces also come into play with inspired thinking, which may be attained through a number of different spiritual disciplines, including meditation. Or, more direct approaches may be used for contacting the imaginative forces, such as music reverie or Jung's technique called active imagination.

2. The unconscious will can lead us into *instructive life situations* and *synchronistic events* that point toward a solution. In other words, life itself becomes the teacher, with the unconscious will leading the way.

Haven't we all experienced this kind of guidance, no matter how we may have understood or interpreted it at the time? In a period of confusion, you may have found yourself coincidentally picking up a magazine that contains an article addressing your problem. Or, just when you had to make an important decision, you unexpectedly ran into an old friend in a shopping mall, only to discover that she recently went through the same challenging situation and has some good advice to share. What stands behind these sorts of synchronistic encounters which offer guidance? One way of understanding them is to recognize that the unconscious will—with its wisdom *and* its innate capabilities for unconscious ESP—can subtly lead the conscious self to just the right place at just the right time in order to meet these instructive situations.

However, both of these activities—imagination and synchronistic events—can be blocked or overshadowed by a Realm #2 will which is preoccupied with the final solution it has already formulated. We must achieve a kind of openness and flexibility in our conscious life of willing. Then Realm #1 will can reveal its ways to us through imaginative possibilities and the circumstances of life. What is needed is a delicate balance which still allows Realm #2 will to do certain things regarding the dilemma without assuming that the whole matter rests with its achievements.

With this ideal in mind, let's consider a nine-step program for getting guidance and making decisions which respects both realms of the will. The following nine-step technique is one framework in which to experience such a creative balance:

Step 1. Set your spiritual ideal. The simple procedure for setting a spiritual ideal was described in Exercise #11 of Chapter 5, and it will be more fully described in Chapter 9. Remember that it involves the conscious choice of an overall life direction. In a single word or a phrase, you have described the spirit you would like to have guiding and directing every aspect of your life. It is something to which you aspire in your spiritual growth, even if you rarely measure up to it now. Examples include "peaceful centeredness," "joyous service," and "oneness with the Christ spirit," just to name a few of almost countless possible wordings. Recall what you have chosen as most meaningful to you personally.

Step 2. Feel the readiness of a question to be answered. The next seven steps can be successful only if the question you pose is one you are ready to have answered. In other words, there is a rightness of timing for virtually any life challenge. You, the seeker, must be sensitive to when a question is still in the process of emerging and when the timing is right for an answer. When you feel really ready to learn what is the best way to approach some problem, then the time is right to proceed to the third step.

Step 3. Carefully formulate a wording for the question. At Step 2, the challenge or difficulty may still be somewhat vague, but at this third step, you must formulate a specific wording for the issue. On paper, write out what you seek to know. Clarify for yourself whether you're looking for a direct answer, more information, or confirmation of something you're already inclined to do.

Step 4. Consider all the factors bearing on this question that you have some current knowledge about. This step involves working with the conscious mind to list all information relevant to your question. Suppose your question was: "Should I move to Arizona?" In this fourth step, you would list all relevant information you already have, such as feelings of other family members about a move, job prospects in Arizona, considerations concerning the climate, local cost of living, etc.

Step 5. Arrive at a tentative conscious decision. Using rational common sense as well as your own feelings, weigh all the factors listed in Step 4, and formulate a preliminary answer to your question. Make sure that the tentative answer is in keeping with your spiritual ideal. Additional steps follow this one, but you need to feel good enough about your tentative answer to follow through on it without compromising your ideal.

Step 6. Obtain guidance from "outer sources" concerning your tentative decision. At this stage, you may want to turn to a trusted friend or professional counselor for advice. Or, you may want to use such esoteric resources as psychic readings, astrological readings, numerology, or I Ching. Another form of outer guidance you may find helpful is the periodic occurrence of synchronistic signs and life events which contain a quality of guidance. Here is the first place where the unconscious will—Realm #1—may start to come into play. By themselves, such meaningful coincidences may not be a reliable source upon which to base an important decision. Yet once you have arrived at a tentative conscious answer (i.e., Step 5), synchronistic events may give you a feeling of confirmation or warning. As mentioned earlier, these coincidental signs may take the form of things you read, hear about or see, which, in an inexplicable way, seem to provide you with feedback on the issue which concerns you.

For this sixth step, work only with those forms of outer guidance with which you feel comfortable. Individuals may differ widely in their choice of outer resources.

Step 7. Look for guidance coming from "inner resources." Many different avenues are available to each of us for tuning in to a higher wisdom and higher will. Some people receive these inner promptings through imaginative reverie; others find that dreams provide such guidance. But no matter what other avenues may be pursued, be sure to include meditation guidance as a resource. Here is a direct way to encounter Realm #1 will.

Using meditation to receive guidance is quite simple. However, you must not use your question as a kind of mantra or affirmation, but rather you would complete a period of attunement (including prayer for others) *before* turning to the question or problem at hand. In other words, take several minutes at the end of your meditation period to pose quietly in your conscious mind the question you formulated (i.e., in Step 3 above). Hold the question in mind and feel your sincere desire to resolve this issue. Experience your openness to understand the question in a new light. Feel a readiness to make whatever required changes a deeper wisdom within you may suggest.

After silently posing and contemplating the question, begin to *listen*. The listening must be broader than merely listening for a voice, no matter how still or small. In fact, some people do receive guidance through an inward kind of hearing (hence, clairaudience as one form of psychic perception). However, most people receive their guidance in some way other than by actually hearing words. The listening process should encompass one's whole being. Listen with your body. Listen with your imaginative forces. Listen with that part of your mind which formulates new concepts and ideas.

What should you expect to receive? Although individuals differ widely in how they experience guidance, people report the following types of inner response:

• A *feedback* feeling or intuition of the rightness or wrongness of the tentative conscious answer (i.e., feedback on what was consciously decided at Step 5).

- A strong feeling, intuition, or image of what is likely to happen if the tentative decision is followed. In this case, the unconscious will is not making any decision, but *precognitively* giving impressions of likely future events, leaving it to the conscious will to decide whether or not that is the desired result.

- A new, previously unconsidered *solution*. Although we may often hope for this result in seeking meditation guidance, it is not necessarily the most frequent result. A direct answer or solution is sometimes presented, but often it is merely a piece of the puzzle with the remaining parts left to be filled in by the conscious self. By way of analogy, imagine that you have asked a skilled mathematician to be your tutor in a difficult algebra course. Now you are stumped on one particular problem. The tutor doesn't provide you with the entire solution, but gives you a piece of the answer to get you started on finding the rest of the solution for yourself. Your unconscious will may work the same way.

- Impressions which provide a *new perspective* on the current question or problem. In other words, the insight received in meditation may now answer the problem but, instead, suddenly allow you to see the question from a new angle. Sometimes this new view can then quickly lead to understanding the appropriate way to respond.

- Recognition of *another question* to be dealt with *before* the original issue can be addressed. In other words, you may have posed a question you sincerely desire to have answered, and yet there are other issues to be resolved first. Suppose you've posed this question: "Should I go back to graduate school to obtain further job skills?" In meditation, you may receive impressions not directly concerned with an answer to this question, but instead you may call to mind other questions that must be resolved first, such as "Are you making the best use of the skills you currently have?" "Have you resolved how you contribute to the dissatisfaction you feel with your current job situation?"

It is highly recommended that before moving on to the next step, you seek meditation guidance more than once, particularly for an issue of great personal importance.

Step 8. Formulate a "guided" decision upon which you are ready to act. Take into account the input provided from both outer sources of guidance as well as inner guidance such as meditation. Then reconsider the question and write down a revised version of your answer—one that you're ready to begin to apply. Make sure this decision is something you could conceivably follow through on and still be in keeping with your spiritual ideal.

Step 9. Begin to apply the decision and yet respond constructively to obstacles which may arise. Almost invariably, when you begin to put into motion a decision (no matter how meditatively you may have arrived at it), obstacles and resistances arise. Sometimes these obstacles can be traced directly to an origin within yourself, although most frequently you experience them as coming from outside. Of course, the hope is that the guided decision will be easy to bring to fruition. Yet seldom is this the case.

When such obstacles arise, you are likely to respond in one of two nonproductive ways:

First, you may tend to try bullheadedly to force your way through the obstacles. Something within you says, "I've gotten my guidance and now I'm going to *make* it happen, no matter what anyone else says or does!" This kind of stubbornness very rarely leads to a happy ending. The mistaken use here is an overactivity of Realm #2 will.

The second frequent response is to give up. Something within you expects that everything should quickly fall into place, if you have tuned into a higher wisdom. This lazy part of yourself doesn't want to have to make any persistent efforts.

A third alternative is better. It requires a willingness to persist with the conscious will in applying the guided decision. But it also requires a continued openness to the unconscious will, so that the obstacles or resistances can *teach* you and help you to *refine* the guidance. Think of it this way: Through guidance counseling, psychic readings, dreams, meditation or any other forms of guidance, you may have the basic *theme* of the best decision, yet not have a proper understanding of the right *timing* or *way* in which to proceed, or of the *people* who will be involved in bringing the decision to fruition.

The best approach carefully blends (a) consistent effort with (b) an open-mindedness that looks upon guidance as an *ongoing process* and not something that was resolved once and for all in Step 8. You must let life continue to instruct you. Continue to pay attention to your dreams and imaginative insights. Watch how your unconscious will may lead you into instructive situations. Continue to seek meditation guidance, even as you are already acting on your guided decision.

You are invited to experiment with this program in your own decision making. Think of yourself as a spiritual researcher and try following these nine steps. Like any good research project, it may take some time. Don't expect this carefully constructed program to be a quick-fix shortcut. For some decisions, it may even take several weeks to complete all phases of the procedure. But you can be assured that you will have followed a program that leaves room for both sides of your will.

RECOMMENDED ADDITIONAL READING

The Ways of Will, Leslie Farber (Basic Books, New York, 1966)

The first chapter is especially important reading: "The Two Realms of Will." The book is out of print and you will have to search libraries to find it.

Discover the wealth of information in the Edgar Cayce readings

Dreams
Soul Mates
Karma
Earth Changes
Universal Laws
Meditation
Holistic Health
ESP
Astrology
Atlantis
Psychic Development
Numerology
Pyramids
Death and Dying
Auto-Suggestion
Reincarnation
Akashic Records
Planetary Sojourns
Mysticism
Spiritual Healing
And other topics

Membership Benefits You Receive Each Month

EDGAR CAYCE FOUNDATION and
A.R.E. LIBRARY/VISITORS CENTER
Virginia Beach, Va.
OVER 50 YEARS OF SERVICE

NO POSTAGE
NECESSARY
IF MAILED
IN THE
UNITED STATES

BUSINESS REPLY CARD
First Class Permit No. 2456, Virginia Beach, Va.

POSTAGE WILL BE PAID BY

A.R.E.®
P.O. Box 595
Virginia Beach, VA 23451

PART THREE

Living Your Life with Good Will

CHAPTER SEVEN

A Model of
Mind and Will

The purpose of a model is twofold. First, it helps us organize our ideas about a topic. By systematically arranging what we know into a cohesive picture, we can get a better hold on what might otherwise be merely scattered observations. Second, a model helps us to predict, to look ahead, and see what our future experiences may be. In physics or chemistry, a model of natural laws can not only help the scientist grasp the meaning of his observations, but can also assist him in making hypotheses for future experiments. The same process can work for us in regard to our study of the will and its relationship to the mind.

No model can explain everything. For example, in drawing a two-dimensional diagram to summarize relationships among three- or four-dimensional things, certain important features must be lost. The very characteristic that makes a model handy—its simplicity— is also its limitation. In other words, we should not expect too much from any model. It is only natural that we find exceptions that don't fit the model, particularly when the model is trying to represent in the limitations of two dimensions the nature of a reality of far greater complexity.

With these reservations stated in advance, we can move ahead and explore a model to depict the relationship between mind and will. The diagram we shall develop is based on the principle that mind and will are in direct opposition to each other. This fundamental tension is proposed both in the Cayce readings ("Mind is the factor that is in direct opposition of will"—3744-1) and in the lectures of Steiner ("Antipathy on the one hand changes our soul life into [mental] picture images: sympathy, which goes in the other direction, changes our soul life into what we know as our will . . ."—*Study of Man*, p. 31).

The many examples already given suggest the truth of this inherent opposition. There is a recurrent tension between mind and will to shape your sense of personal identity. Your will is an active principle which can orient your identity toward the *future*, your destiny in spiritual evolution. As your will awakens and becomes active, your mind more and more becomes subservient to it. Yet even then your mind retains the tendency to go back to the old and familiar patterns. If your will momentarily falls asleep, your mind takes the lead again.

On the one hand, opposition sounds like a discouraging notion. It suggests that mind and will are doomed always to compete and to be at war with each other. It seems to imply that each of us is stuck with a kind of internal conflict that cannot be remedied.

On the other hand, there is a more hopeful way of viewing this principle. This sort of tension is part of the way we are built, but it can be viewed in a positive way: It is a creative tension. Just as there would be no electricity to cook our food or heat our water without positive and negative electrical forces, there might not be spiritual evolution for human souls without a creative polarity that can be used to propel us forward.

So we construct our model of the mind and will by starting with this basic principle of opposition. It can be represented as two axes. This is not a polar tension (i.e., not a "tug-of-war" on the same rope from its two ends) but rather a so-called "orthogonal opposition."

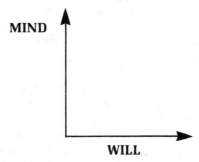

From high school mathematics, you may remember drawing graphs of algebraic expressions which could be depicted on axes like these, although they were not labeled "mind" and "will." This two-dimensional skeleton of a model can be used to represent relationships and experiences. But let's start with something far more mundane and then later move to this fundamental creative tension of the human soul. Consider the simple example of heat and humidity, something we become particularly aware of in the middle of the summer.

Suppose we label the horizontal axis "heat" and the vertical axis "humidity."

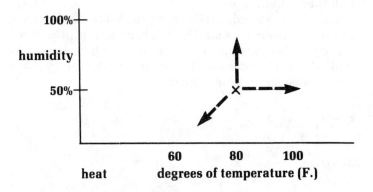

The "x" on the diagram represents the experience of being in a room with a temperature of 80°F. and a humidity of 50%. Each of the three dotted arrows depicts how our experience of heat and humidity could be altered. The horizontal arrow on our model shows a movement created by rising temperature with no change in humidity—which would happen in the room if we drew back the curtains to permit some solar heating. The vertical arrow shows an increase in humidity with no change in temperature— which would happen if we sprayed a mist of 80°F. temperature water in the room. Finally, the diagonal dotted arrow represents decreasing temperature accompanied by decreasing humidity—which would happen if we turned on the air-conditioning system.

In a similar fashion, we can depict specific conditions of human experience. Instead of degrees of temperature, we shall be concerned with stages of will development. Instead of the percent humidity, we shall focus on the expansiveness of mind, ranging from unlimited, universal mind to the rather confined state we call the three-dimensional, physical conscious mind.

In the diagram below, the axes are labeled and some points of measurement along each have been added. The indication of " ∞ " at the top of the mind scale means infinite or divine mind. Of course, the infinite is not a point along a line, but for the limited purposes of our model, we can think of the top extremity of the vertical axis as unlimited, divine mind.

The point labeled "3-D" means the three-dimensional, physical conscious mind. The unlabeled region in between represents various dimensions of mind which are not as limited as our typical conscious mind but which do not have the expansiveness of infinite mind.

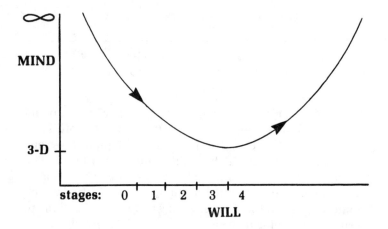

The curving line depicts the creation story. Souls were created with infinite mind, but the *will* was only an unawakened potential—like a present or gift that had been given but was yet unopened. Souls were one with God, but they did not know it; it was unconscious oneness. The purpose of the soul's journey is to become something even better than it was at creation. Since the beginning, each soul has had laid before it a Plan whereby, through the awakening of the will and through the awakening of the sense of individual identity, it can become a co-creative companion with God.

The curving line represents the Plan. It was with great purposefulness that each of us started out upon that journey. We did not end up carefully following the Plan, and we must now realign ourselves with it. But before we examine the current human condition, let us get a clear image of the intention of the original Plan.

In the beginning we were in a state of oceanic, unconscious oneness with the Creator. A similar state was re-experienced by each of us just after our physical birth in this lifetime. As infants we had a kind of oceanic oneness, especially with Mother or our primary caretaker. But what happened next, hundreds of thousands of years ago? What was needed in order for us to get started on a spiritual maturation process? The oceanic, universal mind was overwhelming. As long as we stayed in that state, the unique personal will could never have awakened. We would never have come to realize our freedom and our individuality.

We were meant to move temporarily into more and more limited states of mind, but with an ever-increasing sense of our own unique, individual nature. As mind became more limited, the personal will awakened and expanded. Notice on the model diagram how the left-hand side of the parabolic curve moves downward (more limited mind) and to the right (more awakened will). A point was to be reached—the lowest point of the parabola—where the will is so awakened in a personal way that we can move yet another step—into transpersonal will. Notice how the turning point on the curve corresponds to the transition along the will scale from Stage 3 to Stage 4.

Once the Real Will begins to direct us, then the higher states of mind can once again be attained. The goal of the journey is to attain a mind as unlimited and divine as that which we had in the beginning, but now with a fully developed sense of individuality. Truly, we can then be co-creative companions with God.

The themes of this story of creation are better known to us in the fairy tale of *Pinocchio*, particularly in the modern version created by a master myth-maker of our age, Walt Disney. Often a myth, story or parable can better capture those aspects of truth which do not lend themselves easily to rational explanation. They also can be retained more easily because of the vividness of their imagery.

Pinocchio is the story of each one of us and the journey of the soul's evolution. The wooden Pinocchio is created by male and female divinity figures. First, Geppetto carves Pinocchio's body out of a piece of wood. Then, the magical Blue Fairy appears and she bestows life on Pinocchio. In addition, she places in Pinocchio's life a kind of inner wisdom or spiritual consciousness in the form of a transformed cricket. By touching Jiminy Cricket on the top of his head (perhaps symbolic of the crown chakra or pineal gland center), the Blue Fairy commissions him to stay always with Pinocchio in order to guide him.

Geppetto is overjoyed at having a living puppet. But somehow things aren't quite good enough. He marvels at his creation, but he wishes that Pinocchio could become something even better. Gepetto desires an "amelioration" —that things would get better. So the next day Pinocchio is sent off to school in order to learn what he needs to know. He wants to qualify to become a *real boy*. It's crucial to note here that Pinocchio does *not* run away, but instead it is Geppetto who *encourages his departure* because it is part of a plan for Pinocchio's improvement.

However, once Pinocchio is away from home, he begins to misuse his new-found freedom. In this sense, Pinocchio *does* experience a Fall, but it is not at the point of leaving the father's home. Instead, the great error comes once he is out on his own. He succumbs to the temptation of evil figures despite the protestations of Jiminy Cricket. First, he is enticed by a carnival show operator named Stromboli to show off on stage. But this episode in vanity ends with Pinocchio's imprisonment in a cage. The Blue Fairy comes to his rescue and he is released, but only after a scene in which he *lies* to the Blue Fairy and is shocked to see that those lies manifest in his physical appearance: his nose grows longer. This illustrates that when the human will falls prey to evil, a natural result is to lie.

Next, Pinocchio succumbs to the temptations of a fox named Honest John. Again Pinocchio chooses to ignore Jiminy Cricket, his conscience, and is led into a series of misadventures. He is enticed to visit Pleasure Island, a place of total physical indulgence. After an initial good time, Pinocchio is horrified to see that he and the other boys are starting to turn into animals. They grow ears and tails like donkeys, and are shocked to see other boys who have been completely transformed into this animal state. Here is graphic symbology of the soul having indulged itself in material life and having forgotten its real nature. The soul begins to assume the consciousness of an animal form. The willful, stubborn donkey is an especially appropriate image in the fairy tale, calling attention as it does to the role of the will.

Fortunately, Pinocchio is able to escape from Pleasure Island by following the lead of Jiminy Cricket. Pinocchio then resolves to return to his father, but he soon discovers that his father is also out looking for him. Through guidance, Pinocchio learns that his father can be found deep beneath the sea (i.e., it is within the depths of the unconscious that our spiritual origins can be re-encountered). In fact, Geppetto is to be found in the belly of the great "fish"—a whale named Monstro.

Through persistent searching and a little luck, Pinocchio finds his father inside the great "fish." Despite the joy of this reunion, a problem remains. How are they to bring this reunion up out of the depths of the sea and into the safety of dry land and their home? In other words, we may now begin to have a re-union with God in the depths of our unconscious life (e.g., in dreams, in meditation). But how are we to bring this reunion into the light of day, into waking consciousness and physical life? With great creative insight and courage, Pinocchio and his father escape from their underwater prison, but only at a great price. Geppetto tires in the escape and Pinocchio sacrifices himself to make sure that his father makes it safely to shore. Geppetto awakens on the beach only to find the apparently lifeless body of his wooden puppet Pinocchio.

Dutifully he takes him home and carefully lays him in a bed. But the Blue Fairy has been drawn back because of Pinocchio's love, courage, and self-sacrifice. Touching him, she resuscitates him. The resurrected Pinocchio is no longer a living, wooden puppet. He has been ameliorated, and now he is the *real boy* for whom Geppetto had first wished. This happy conclusion represents a point in the soul's evolution which is still in our own future. It is a point at which we shall become conscious, co-creative companions with God—something even better than what we were in the beginning.

But let's consider how this story, depicting *our own* errors along the Path, could be represented on the model diagram. This story admits that a mistake was made; however, it was not at the beginning, when the soul first made a movement toward a more limited state of mind. Instead, it was part of the Plan that we experience limited states of mind. An error took place when we continued to move toward ever more limited states of mind while starting to *weaken* rather than strengthen the personal will. Notice below how the small curved arrow shows this kind of movement: deeper into mental limitation but regressing in terms of will development.

We might interpret what occurred thousands of years ago in the following manner:

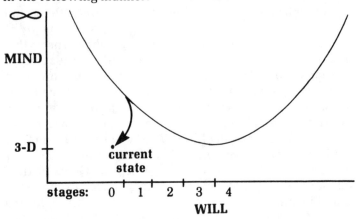

In using the mind this way, souls created images which began to have a hypnotic effect. The newly emerging will was now weakened. The souls fell "asleep" in what they had created, forgetting their individualities as souls and believing their identities to be something far less.

They moved into limited states of mind in which they could more readily feel their individual nature. But in so doing, they found themselves in a place where they could use their newly awakening will to create mental images to satisfy selfish ends. In other words, they discovered both their freedom and the power of mind. They experienced *directly and vividly* that thoughts are things. But many of these mental creations were selfish and indulgent.

The readings given by Cayce on this subject are among the most difficult to interpret of all his material. Yet one interesting note is that a soul named Amelius is described as having led large numbers of souls into the limiting dimensions of physical consciousness. If one thinks about the similarity between that name and the verb "to ameliorate" (i.e., to make better), then there is a clue to the purpose of humanity in the earth plane. For the Cayce readings, the meaning of life is to grow and develop so that we can eventually reach a state described by these words: to know ourselves to be ourselves (i.e., full, self-conscious individuality), yet one with the whole.

Steiner's rendition of creation and soul evolution is presented in several places among his works, including *Cosmic Memory* and *The Gospel of St. John*. Consider, for example, just a few passages from Steiner's esoteric interpretation of that fourth gospel. Although his lectures on this subject are extraordinarily complex and rich, even these few passages can convey the overall thrust of his view: that there is great spiritual meaning to physical life and to the self-conscious individual.

> ... the human being was destined for self-conscious love upon the earth. (p. 54)

> . . . a truly genuine self-consciousness, such as should be acquired during life upon the earth, can only be attained by submersion in a physical body. (p. 46)

On the one hand men had to descend to the lowest level in order that they might become independent and on the other hand a strong force must come which can give again the impulse for finding the path back to the Universal. (p. 86)

So we, as souls, find ourselves today in a peculiar state. We have descended into three-dimensional conscious minds and bodies. In a sense, we were meant to do so. There was a work for us to do here: to bring the qualities of spirit into matter, the finite with the infinite. However, when we reached this state of mind, we were meant to have quite a different state of will than, in fact, we do. Our experience in matter has not turned out the way it was intended, largely because we now live in a sleep-like state (the great faculties of the soul, such as the will, are slumbering) and because we have a mistaken notion of who we are.

So we are left with the question of how to get back on the Path. Psychologically speaking, the Path is like a great stream of archetypal images and universal patterns of consciousness. The myths and parables which have a spiritually quickening impact on us are the ones which are attuned to this great psychic roadway. With the creation of a Divine Plan for the evolution of souls, that Plan took the form of universal images within the unconscious of every soul. In a sense, they are like road markers to confirm for us that we are on the right track. Furthermore, their symbolic quality goes beyond just being confirmatory signs; they also contain a mystery or a tension which provides the energy to move on and evolve further. In other words, archetypal symbols (which may be encountered in meditation or in dreams) serve not only as confirming signposts, but they also exert an ordering, directing influence toward the state of wholeness which Jung called individuation.

What can we do to put ourselves back in the flow of that Path? There may be many routes back to it, but one is most direct. On our model diagram it is a 45° diagonal line. It represents a balanced effort to achieve higher states of mind along with a healthier, more awakened will. It is illustrated as a dotted line, advancing upward, in this figure:

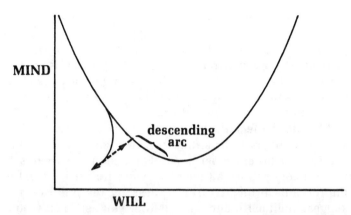

One other feature of the route back should be noted, because it is an experience which troubles so many seekers. Note on the model a curious phenomenon which occurs. Once you have re-established a point of experiencing that is in attunement with the images and archetypes of the Path, there is a movement "downward," relatively speaking. Of course, words such as "up" and "down" are highly misleading in this case. Instead, we might describe this "descending arc" along the parabola as a period in which the will is continuing to awaken but the mind becomes less and less inclined to provide experiences of higher dimensional reality.

Many seekers have gone through such a period in their lives—perhaps more than once, because we continually veer off the Path only to have to work our way back to It again. This "descending arc" is a crucial stage because of the likelihood that you may become discouraged. Out of such discouragement, you may cease to seek and just give up. The mistake that is made involves equating progress along the Path with *only* the dimension of mind, forgetting that our model is two dimensional and requires a growth of will also.

During the period of the "descending arc," life continues to present special challenges and opportunities which shall allow the sense of individuality to emerge, but at the expense of personality. In order for this to happen effectively, a period is needed in which altered states of *mind* are *not* readily available. The higher states of mind can re-emerge further along the Path, but at that future point they will serve the individuality and sense of soul mission. If they were readily available during this crucial period of the "descending arc," they might only take you back into a false feeling of yourself and make the necessary development of will more difficult.

What does it feel like to be in a period of the "descending arc"? It is likely to be a time in which you find it hard to meditate or to remember hopeful and inspiring dreams. It is, for many people, a time of outward failure—when the impressions brought to awareness by the mind do not suggest the health and success that you assumed would come with consistent seeking. For some people, it is a time of becoming physically sick. Even though the symptoms may resemble a typical illness, such a sickness comes for a different purpose. Whatever form the "descending arc" takes in your lives, its purpose is to bring you to the point of *surrender*. But the surrender is not a "giving up motivated by doubt" but rather a "letting go based on hope." The "descending arc" ends when we move into the realm of Real Will—Stage 4 will. At that point you turn a corner, and the purpose for this difficult period in the spiritual quest is accomplished.

The question naturally arises, "Where am I on the model?" The answer consists not in a simple point but rather many points, because each of us spends different parts of the day at different positions in relation to mind and will.

For example, most of us spend the largest part of waking life in the limited state of mind we call three-dimensional consciousness, right on the line between Stage 0 and Stage 1 of will—usually "asleep" in life and struggling just to say "no" occasionally. This point has been depicted in the model as the tip of the detour arrow, which illustrates our departure from the Plan. But we may have moments in the day of heightened mind and/or increased functionings of the will. As we progress on this spiritual quest, we begin to spend more and more of our lives experiencing greater individuality and co-creativity.

Ultimately our goal is to have a permanent state of consciousness that would be represented in the upper right-hand corner of the model diagram: infinite, universal mind combined with the highest Transpersonal (or Real) Will. But while we are in a physical body in the earth—still incarnate—there is a different ideal state: to be right at the turning point of the parabola curve.

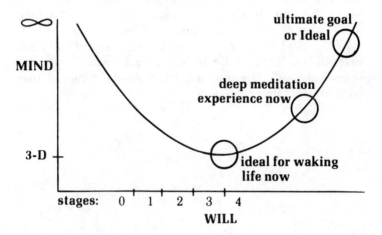

That turning point corresponds to (1) a mind fully functioning with the awareness of physical reality and (2) a will that is right on the border between Stage 3 and Stage 4. This means a will which is strong and empowering at a personal level—a will that has fully awakened the seven qualities described in Chapter 3. But it is also a spot from which the will can readily surrender to a Higher Will. It is a state of personal will development that is equally capable of great personal accomplishment or authentic obedience to the promptings of the Spirit.

We should, of course, add the experience of deep meditation to the list of ideal states on the model diagram. In these moments we feel directed by Transpersonal Will *and* there is the presence of an altered state of mind. These experiences are invaluable because they help us to be more sensitive to the highest form of will throughout the rest of the day.

In summary, then, this model can serve as a useful way of organizing our thinking about the spiritual path. In spite of certain limitations in the model, it represents key principles. It graphically illustrates how the purpose of physical life is positive, how we are growing into something we have never yet been. The model also helps us see how we may have recurrent periods of struggle, which really do involve growth despite appearances. These times along the descending arc are especially times in which awakening of the will forces is possible.

In the next chapter we examine more specifically the essential challenge of life: to deal correctly with the powers of good and evil. The human will is right at the heart of that paradoxical power struggle.

RECOMMENDED ADDITIONAL READING

Up from Eden, Ken Wilber (Anchor Press, Garden City, N.Y., 1981)

This is an extraordinary book of highly documented comparisons about the development of human consciousness over the millennia. Although it is not easy reading, it is probably the best book available on the subject. Wilber synthesizes dozens of sources and makes a strong case for distinct stages in the evolution of consciousness.

The Essential Steiner, Robert McDermott, editor (Harper and Row, San Francisco, 1984)

Section 3 of this anthology presents a sampling of Steiner's own lectures on human history. Steiner's notion of the seven post-Atlantean cultural epochs fits the model of a descending, then re-ascending, parabola.

Man and World in the Light of Anthroposophy, Stewart Easton (Anthroposophic Press, Spring Valley, N.Y., 1975)

This is for those who prefer to read a scholar's in-depth summary of Steiner's model of human history rather than Steiner's own lectures. Chapter 2 tells the story in great detail.

CHAPTER EIGHT

The Role of Will in the Powers of Good and Evil

Why study a subject as distasteful as evil? Why focus on one of the least hopeful issues facing humanity today—the pervasive and destructive influence of evil? The answer lies with the following assertion: For the ideas in this book to have any authentic, lasting value, they must lead you to an experience of your own *good will.*

What does this familiar phrase—*good will*—mean? You probably hear it more often in daily life than you hear references to the *will* alone. For example:

Her gesture expressed good will.

Peace on earth, good will toward men.

The diplomats argued, but there remained a good will between them.

That simple phrase—good will—conveys so much. It means sincerity and openness. It speaks of love and compassion. It can overcome our confusion about the paradox of power.

This is the purpose for having a willing spirit. When you move in your life from a sleeping will or willfulness to a willing spirit, then you are in touch with the deepest meaning of life. Perhaps this is precisely what it means to say that the *whole* of your soul development rests with your will. The Spirit itself can live through an awakened, healthy will. When It does, genuine goodness comes to life. Good will.

But it isn't honest to pretend that there is only good. It denies immediate human experience to say that evil doesn't really exist, to say that it's only a delusion because everything is actually perfect. Such a denial is also inconsistent with the teachings of the Christ. (The easiest example to find is the Lord's Prayer taught by Jesus, which contains references to both temptation and evil.) Instead, an honest approach to life recognizes that evil and sin are real. A willing spirit and good will do not exist without the possibility for willful dispiritedness and ill will.

The most ancient *and* the most pressing modern problem for humanity is the question of evil. According to the mythic wisdom of Genesis, no sooner were man and woman created than they fell prey to temptation. By their rebellious act of going against God's will, they came to "the knowledge of good and evil," and the history of human struggle began. In today's world there is no place we can turn without having to confront the presence of evil and being forced to make decisions in response to its influence. Our world has probably always been plagued with problems like crime, greed, child abuse, and terrorism, but now we are bombarded daily with national and international reports on the faces of evil. Numbed by the sheer volume of its evidence, we find it extremely difficult to see how the response of one person can make much of a difference.

The purpose of this chapter is twofold. The first addresses this question: Has our thorough study of the nature of will equipped us to address the problem of good and evil with fresh insight? In other words, could it be that the will itself is so integrally a part of the problem of evil that an in-depth study of the will has indirectly provided us with a new understanding of evil?

The second purpose of this chapter is to explore what is perhaps the most important human arena in which a healthy will can be applied. Our study must be something more than just a theoretical exercise. We should have a good reason for our personal work awakening and training the will. By analogy, we can think of the countless numbers of people who are devoted to aerobic or weight-training programs at health clubs. Despite all the effort, how many of them have a clear reason for achieving a body with greater strength or stamina? How many of them have a higher purpose in mind which their new body will allow them to serve? The same kind of question should be asked of will training. But in this case there is a good answer: A more healthy will can allow us to meet more directly and creatively the problem of evil within ourselves and in the world around us.

The problem of evil and its relationship to the good is truly one of the great human questions. It is not possible to answer that question in a space so brief as this chapter, or perhaps even in volumes of books. In fact, the mystery of good and evil is a fundamental paradox with which every human wrestles. Nowhere is the paradox of power directly encountered. But rather than try to resolve the question once and for all, we are probably wiser to let the mystery continually challenge and teach us. An awakened and healthy human will makes that possible.

The psychiatrist M. Scott Peck proposes a useful definition of evil: "the imposition of one's will upon others by overt or covert coercion—in order to avoid spiritual growth." In other words, the misuse of the will is a central characteristic of evil. The problem of evil lies in the will itself.

One of the most fascinating aspects of Peck's work is the set of models which he outlines. Recognizing that people have not always agreed about the nature of evil, he describes these major theological models.

1. The non-dualism of Hinduism and Buddhism. With this model there is oneness so fundamental that evil is just the other side of the coin from good. Distinguishing evil from good is illusory since they are part of the same whole: life must have death, growth must have decay, creation must have destruction. Peck feels that this attitude toward evil has crept into some spiritual teachings which claim to be Christian or Christ-centered, but he is skeptical about the soundness of trying to blend the two. The examples he cites are Christian Science and *A Course in Miracles*.

2. Integrated dualism has some of the features of the first model but more clearly distinguishes evil from good. Here

the two sides are different, but they are meaningfully
related, and both are the creation of God. In this model, evil
plays a critical role in human spiritual development.
Having created us with free will, God permits evil because
it requires the choices by which we learn to use the will in
accordance with the highest Good.

3. Diabolical dualism is the model of traditional
Christianity. In this model, evil is viewed as outside of
God's creation and a hideous problem beyond His control.
Presumably the only possible control rests with how each
individual uses his or her free will to meet the temptations
of evil. But this model has its own shortcomings (for
example, *who* or *what* created evil if it was not part of God's
plan?).

As is often the case when the best thinkers of human
history have arrived at different answers to a question, the
greatest truth probably lies in some type of composite of all
of them. This principle is clearly illustrated in the study of
light. There is evidence to support a model of light, showing
its nature to be particles called photons. But there is also a
model and supportive evidence demonstrating that light is
instead made up of vibrating waves. Paradoxically, both
are true. In a similar fashion, there is probably some truth in
all three models of evil.

Nevertheless, the second model is the one with which we
can best work: integrated dualism. In other words, let's
explore a profound *middle ground* between (1) non-
dualism that ignores the distinctiveness of evil and (3)
diabolical dualism that bestows evil with a separate
power.

Even though there are forces of good and evil throughout
the universe, the real point of our concern should be the
interplay of these influences *within* us. Rather than blame
another person or the Devil for our difficulties, we can
instead discover that all the goodness and all the evil we can
know is also found within ourselves.

But how do we encounter evil? In our choices. In our
opportunities to use will. This ancient idea is found in the
Old Testament: "See, I have set before thee this day life and

good, and death and evil . . . choose life . . ." (Deuteronomy 30:15, 19) It is the capacity to choose between good and evil which makes each member of humanity a spiritual being instead of a robot. In other words, without the presence of evil to force the exercising of free will, there would be no prospect for human spiritual development. This idea is the very essence of integrated dualism.

The model of integrated dualism makes possible a radical view of the relationship between good and evil. Even if there is a fundamental oneness to life, it should not cause us to blur distinctions between these two influences. Good is real, and so is evil. However, they are not irreconcilable opposites. In keeping with the spirit of *integrated* dualism, evil (or "bad") is something just under good. It is goodness which is merely twisted but which can be redeemed through the wise application of human will. Bad is only good gone wrong.

For example, suppose you have the bad habit of being impatient with projects which don't go as planned. Contained within the impatience is the seed of something good—high ideals and determination to see things done right. Or, suppose you have a bad habit of manipulating people. That is not a good habit. It needs to be changed. However, embedded within the habit is the essence of something good. You are a good motivator of people. Unfortunately, that good trait has become tainted with your own insecurities or power drives. The innate talent has gotten twisted and comes out looking like this regrettable impulse to coerce people to do what you want. Nevertheless, in both examples, bad is only good gone wrong. As the Cayce readings put it:

> For what is bad? Good gone wrong, or something *else*? It is good misapplied, misconstrued, or used in a *selfish* manner, for the satisfying of a desire within self. 1089-5

> Books, in their essence, are what? What is the more real, the book with its printed pages, its gilt edges, or the essence of that told of in the book? Which is the more real, the love manifested in the Son . . . or the essence of love that may be seen even in the vilest of passion?

They are one . . .

How far, then, is ungodliness from godliness? Just under, that's all!   254-68

The Two Faces of Evil

The Jewish theologian Martin Buber is one of the finest exponents of the integrated dualism model of evil. In this passage from his classic work *Good and Evil* we see these themes addressed:

> In the creation of man, the two urges [i.e., the good urge and the evil urge] are set in opposition to each other. The Creator gives them to man as his two servants which, however, can only accomplish their service in genuine collaboration. The "evil urge" is no less necessary than its companion, indeed even more necessary than it . . . Hence, this urge is called "the yeast in the dough," the ferment placed in the soul by God, without which the human dough does not rise . . .
>
> It [the evil urge] became so [became *evil*], and continually becomes so, because man separates it from its companion and in this condition of independence makes an idol of precisely that which was intended to serve him. Man's task, therefore, is not to extirpate the evil urge, but to reunite it with the good. (*Good and Evil*, pp. 94-95)

This notion of "yeast in the dough" is a crucial one. It is a way of seeing evil (or the urge to evil) as an invaluable growth opportunity. We simply wouldn't grow spiritually without it, because it gives the will something with which to work. Inner development can happen only through inner temptation. But here we must be careful. It's not that we are to use the will to destroy or repress the evil urge. That doesn't lead to authentic growth. Instead, we are to use the will to take that which is bad and unite it with the good.

However, Buber's idea goes further. He distinguishes between a so-called "evil urge," placed in human life by God for a purpose, and "evil" itself. Humanity brings evil into being through a lack of consciousness or a lack of will to deal properly with the "evil urge." In fact, for Buber, there are two stages or faces of evil—two distinct ways in which we fail to deal adequately with the "evil urge" and consequently experience evil.

Buber only rarely refers directly to the will itself in his treatment of good and evil. However, when he writes, "Man repeatedly experiences the dimension of evil as indecision" (p. 134), he opens to us the possibility of interpreting his two stages of evil in terms of a problem with will.

What are these two "urges" placed within us? The so-called evil urge is defined by Buber as *passion*, something which is necessary for human activity in the earth, necessary for any kind of physical creativity. However, this passion, "*left to itself*, remains without direction and leads astray." (p. 97) On the other hand, the good urge is defined as pure direction toward God. Spiritual development rests with the wise use of will to blend these two, so as to equip the potency of passion with the directionality of love and service. The failure to do so brings evil.

The first face of evil is the product of living unconsciously. It is the stage of evil which allows passions to play themselves out without being coupled to God's direction, to an ideal of love and service. In this stage of evil, we act without really having fully decided. This sort of evil is related to will, according to Buber, because it comes from a "partial decision" instead of a decision from the whole soul. Only one side of us decides, *only one* urge is recognized and respected.

To make this more practical, let's consider two examples. There is nothing inherently bad in the sexual urge. But when that passion is given free rein and we rather unconsciously let it control our lives, then it quickly turns to the evil of domination and exploitation. This condition, according to Buber, is a partial decision—a failure of will—because it leaves the complementary force untouched. However, it is possible to blend that sexual urge with the direction of commitment and love. Now the healthy will is at work, and now we are deciding with the whole soul. In so doing, sexuality becomes a healing experience.

In a similar fashion, there is nothing inherently bad about

the urge to make money to earn a living. But if that passion is allowed to control us, it turns to the evil of greed. Our opportunity is to use the will to blend this urge with the good, to give a direction and ideal to one's work so that earning money is done in the context of serving others.

The second face of evil in Buber's analysis results from a kind of human pride. Here the will is clearly used, but with no willingness to submit to something Higher. No longer just ignoring unconsciously the other urge of good, it willfully resists its influence in favor of the evil urge. In this kind of evil, the individual claims for himself the credit for existence. It is a play for consolidating earthly power, a power over ourselves and over others. If we think back to the stages of will development described in Chapter 4, it is as if we are getting stuck at Stage 3 (personally empowering will) and are unwilling to surrender personal authority over to God's will. This produces a more *radical* kind of evil in which violence, greed or exploitation is not merely from passion "without direction," but instead is premeditated and personally willed. Buber writes:

> The first stage does not yet contain a "radical evil"; whatever misdeeds are committed, their commission is not a doing of the deed but a sliding into it. In the second stage evil grows radical, because what man finds in himself is willed. (p. 140)

Let's once again try to make these abstract concepts more practical by looking at the examples in which evil seizes upon the natural urges of being sexual and of earning money for a living. In sexuality a clear difference exists between two kinds of evil. One produces domination and exploitation out of undirected passion. The other produces the same results but is created by a premeditated, willed intention to use sex to assert one's own power over another person. In the same way, we should be able to recognize two distinct kinds of evil in regard to making money. One may produce greed simply out of a passion not tempered by an ideal of love. The other may also appear as greed, but it is produced by a consciously willed intention to use money as a way to assert power over others or as a play for invulnerability and security without a need for something Higher.

So evil itself has two sides, two faces. The search for meaning and genuine power can go astray in two distinct ways. One side of evil is what Rudolf Steiner called Luciferic. Lucifer is the voice of *illusion*. It flatters us and invites us to the illusions of a self-importance and grandeur that we really have not yet achieved. He tempts us to prematurely claim to be God-like. Lucifer would have us abandon the physical realm and drift dreamily in the world of spirit without conscious control. He tries to seduce humanity to revel in illusion and retreat to nonmaterial realms, leaving behind earthly responsibilities. Examples of Luciferic evil include giving free rein to passion without a sense of responsibility, vain egotism, being overwhelmed by psychic/occult experiences or drug-induced states, and the passively receptive states into which we can easily drift when hypnotized by the artificial realities of television.

In contrast, a second face of evil is Ahrimanic (from a Persian god of evil "Ahriman"). Ahriman is the voice of *denial*. It mocks our sense of individual worth and tries to persuade us that we are but random events in a meaning-less world. This cynical kind of evil would tie us to the earth and have us deny the spirit altogether. Ahriman tempts us to believe only in what we can see, touch, taste, hear or smell—to rely solely on physical reality. Examples of Ahrimanic evil include reductionistic, mechanical thinking; the lust for earthly power over others; materialism; and an overwhelming fear of bodily death.

It is the Christ which stands on the middle ground between these two faces of evil. The Christ impulse in our lives allows us to appreciate the appropriate place of the spiritual world *and* the material world. In his extraordinary wood sculpture, created near the end of his life, Steiner shows the Christ as the "representative of mankind" standing between images of Lucifer and Ahriman. One hand of the Christ figure is raised, holding back the influences of Lucifer who would pull humanity into dreamy spiritual worlds without personal responsibility. The other hand of the Christ figure is lowered, holding in abeyance the influence of Ahriman who would tempt humanity to deny everything except material reality. This balancing influence between the two extremes of evil is reminiscent of the passage from the Cayce readings: ". . . yet know that *only* in Him—the Christ—do extremes meet." (2449-1)

To illustrate the nature of these two faces of evil, a model diagram may be useful. Let's return to the parabola image developed in Chapter 7 as a way of showing the soul's spiritual evolution in terms of mind and will. First, let's simplify the parabolic curve into a more basic "V." Then let's reduce the categories of mind from many to just two: (1) a mind which perceives all-encompassing unity and (2) a mind which perceives limitation and separateness. Finally, we can lump together some of the five stages of will development so as to create just three categories: (1) the "sleeping will" state of Stage 0; (2) the three progressive levels of *personal* will development as Stages 1, 2, and 3; and (3) the higher Transpersonal Will of Stage 4. The model will be transformed in this way:

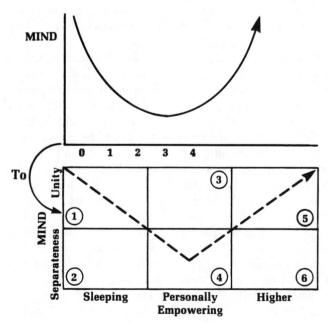

Where, on this revised model, is evil? The great Plan for spiritual evolution is depicted by the dotted arrow that moves through the boxes numbered 1, 4 and 5. What effect would the influence of evil have upon this movement?

Admittedly the question of evil is a complex one and so any efforts to "pin down" the nature of evil on a model as simplistic as this one is bound to have many limitations. Nevertheless, as a tool to get a clearer feeling of the fundamental identity of evil, the following description can be helpful.

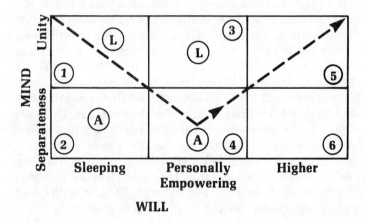

Luciferic evil (indicated by a circled "L") tempts us to move back toward box #1—a place of "sleeping" will and unity of mind. It can be the mass movement or herd consciousness that invites us to get lost in the passions of a collective group. Or it can be the temptation of hallucinogenic drugs which are a de-evolutionary (i.e., regressive) movement toward an ancient kind of oneness.

But Lucifer tempts humanity in *another* way besides going back in consciousness to a place we were long ago. This face of evil also entices us to box #3, which is off the Path and is a place of great illusion. This is the temptation to believe that our own personally empowered identity is godlike. This is the vanity of saying "I am God" with the wrong "I." Luciferic evil assumes that one's own remarkably well-developed and powerful will is the same as God's will.

It is the most basic error of personal growth to mistake the lower aspect of ourselves for the higher one. When we do this, we claim for ourselves something that does not belong to us. For example, it is misleading to ourselves to say "I am God." Most of the time we say this with the wrong "I" and we have fallen under the influence of Luciferic evil. More appropriate to enlightenment is the statement "God is I," which reflects a surrender of self-will and an obedience to a Higher Will and Power.

In contrast, Ahrimanic evil (indicated by a circled "A") tempts us to move off the Path to box #2. This is the familiar fallen state of human consciousness: perceiving life as separation with the mind and being caught in mechanical habit due to a sleeping will. Gurdjieff's Parable of the Horse, Carriage, and Driver (see Chapter 2) provides a good picture of this kind of evil at work. But this is not the only way that the Ahrimanic face of evil entraps us. Once we enter into the work of awakening the personal will, another kind of temptation arises. As personal empower-ment grows with an awakened will, the voice of Ahriman invites us to *stay permanently* in box #4. Here the influence of evil denies that there is anything Higher and, with a cold logic, it nudges us toward a will-for-power.

Will and Evil in the Legend of Faust

All these themes about will and evil are portrayed in the extraordinary story of Faust. The legend of Faust can be traced back at least as far as medieval Europe. It is the account of a man (often described as a magician) who sold his soul to the devil in exchange for supernatural powers. During the Renaissance the legend was given its first significant literary treatment in *The Tragical History of Doctor Faustus* (1588) by the English dramatist Christopher Marlowe. In this rendition, Faust signs a pact with the devil and exchanges 24 years of unlimited power and pleasure for a future in hell. Despite the contract, there is an opportunity provided before his death for Faust to free himself from the devil, *if* his faith in God is strong enough.

But unable to muster sufficient faith and repentance, Faust is carried off by the devil at the conclusion of the play.

A more modern and undoubtedly more famous version of the legend is the epic poem *Faust* by Johann Wolfgang von Goethe. Although not well known to many English-speaking people,* it is generally considered the greatest masterpiece of German literature. Goethe, like those before him, took the rich legend and re-expressed it in a literary vision more suited to his times. Yet Goethe's rendition is still based on the original archetypal themes: the human search for meaning, the role of good and evil in our lives, and the paradox of power.

In an early scene from Goethe's work, the stage is set by a conversation in heaven between God and the devil (called Mephistopheles or Mephisto). They debate how competent a Creator God has been, since humanity seems rather unhappy. God points out the example of the scholar Faust who, despite his current confusion, has a thirst for true knowledge. But Mephisto thinks much less highly of Faust and bets that he can easily lead him astray. Having great faith in his creation, God grants permission for Mephisto to test Faust.

> *Mephisto:* What will you wager? Him you yet shall
> lose,
> If you will give me your permission
> To lead him gently on the Path I choose.

> *The Lord:* As long as on the earth he shall survive,
> So long you'll meet no prohibition.
> Man errs as long as he doth strive . . .
> (Lines 312-317, translated by George
> Madison Priest, Alfred A. Knopf,
> publisher, 1941)

This Doctor Faust who has been selected for the test (much as Job is chosen in the Old Testament story) is no ordinary man. He has a modern, inquiring mind, committed to a spiritual quest for Truth. Because he has a questioning mind, he can be tempted; but because he is sincere and has a

---

*Except perhaps through the popular operatic version of Part I by Charles Gounod.

high ideal, it is possible for him to use his *will* to resist.

Who is this Mephisto? He is the fallen angel, but one whom God permits to influence humanity because it serves His great Plan. What is more, humanity *needs* Mephisto— for without him, we too easily languish in our growth and make no progress. Speaking to Mephisto, God says:

> Mankind's actvity can languish all too easily,
> A man soon loves unhampered rest;
> Hence, gladly I give him a comrade such as you,
> Who stirs and works and must, as devil, do.
>
> (Lines 338-340)

Even Mephisto recognizes the paradox of his nature. He is the liar, the destroyer, the spirit of denial. Yet, despite his nature, he sees how his influence often brings a greater good which wasn't his intention.

> *Faust:* The being of such gentlemen as you, indeed,
> In general, from your titles one can read.
> It shows itself but all too plainly when men dub
> You Liar or Destroyer or Beelzebub.
> Well now, who are you then?
>
> *Mephistopheles:* Part of that Power which would
> The Evil ever do, and ever does the Good.
> *Faust:* A riddle! Say what it implies!
>
> *Mephistopheles:* I am the Spirit that denies!
> And rightly too; for all that doth begin
> Should rightly to destruction run;
> 'Twere better than that nothing were begun.
> Thus everything that you call Sin,
> Destruction—in a word, as Evil represent—
> That is my own, real element.
>
> (Lines 1331-1344)

The riddle or paradox referred to above is the very heart of how Goethe understood evil. The forces of destruction, sin, and denial are not equal in power to those of divine goodness. However, they are part of God's creation and play an irreplaceable role. Mephisto unintentionally acts to nudge humanity toward spiritual wakefulness.

With the stage thus set with the key characters, let's review the basic elements of Goethe's story. Truly a work of epic proportions, the richness of the plot and characterizations cannot be briefly summarized. However, what we *can* do is identify those themes which seem to depict in a mythical way the very same ideas we have already developed concerning free will and evil.

In Part I, we find a discouraged and frustrated 50-year-old scholar who has seemingly taken the human intellect as far as it can go, yet still has not reached Truth and fulfillment. In desperation Faust has turned to magic as a way to at last attain ultimate knowledge. Mephisto has been stalking him in the guise of a dog but has waited for Faust to make the first move. Sensing something mysterious and sinister about the dog, Faust uses his magic to call forth Mephisto.

Now Mephisto's subtle attacks on Faust begin (symbolic of the influence of evil upon all of us). In Goethe's system of thought about human nature, there are three levels: thinking, feeling, and willing. Mephisto first tries to influence the discouraged thinking side of Faust. (Here the Ahrimanic side of evil encourages denial and cynicism.) He taunts Faust and seeks to discourage any hope or commitment to higher values. Then he offers Faust a deal: Agree to become his servant after death, and Mephisto will guarantee all of Faust's desires for the rest of his physical life. Faust accepts the offer, but slightly changes the wording of the deal. He will die and serve Mephisto forever *if* there ever comes a day when he is so satisfied that he wishes the pleasures of that moment to last forever.

> *Faust:* If ever I lay me on a bed of sloth in peace.
> That instant let for me existence cease.
> If ever with lying flattery you can rule me
> So that contented with myself I stay,
> If with enjoyment you can fool me,
> Be that for me the final day!
> That bet I offer!
>
> *Mephistopheles:* Done!

Faust: Another hand-clasp! There!
            If to the moment I shall ever say:
            "Ah, linger on, thou art so fair!"
            Then may you fetters on me lay,
            Then will I perish, then and there!
            Then may the death-bell toll, recalling
            Then from your service you are free;
            The clock may stop, the pointer falling,
            And time itself be past for me!

                                              (Lines 1692-1706)

The agreement now set, Mephisto's attack moves to the second level of Faust's soul—the realm of feeling. Faust is all too ready to be tempted. With his new-found powers, he is eager to taste the emotional sides of life he has missed until now due to his intense search through thinking. Here he is especially susceptible to the Luciferic side of Mephisto—giving free rein to undirected passion. Faust becomes the romantic adventurer under the sway of evil. Through his encounters with Gretchen, his *will fails* to blend the "evil urge" with the "good urge," and passionate lust controls him. This Luciferic evil leads him to revel in the worlds of emotion and egotism, without a sense of responsibility.

Gretchen is a symbol of naive purity. She is tricked into falling in love with Faust and is then seduced by him. As we might expect, behind the scenes is Mephisto. It is *his* power that produces the jewels Faust uses to fascinate Gretchen and to capture her interest. It is Mephisto who keeps reminding Faust of his lust for her whenever Faust has awakenings of genuine love and respect.

In the story, Faust gives to Gretchen a sleeping potion which she administers to her mother in order to make possible a night-time visit by her aroused suitor. Later, we learn of the consequences of their action, again inspired by Mephisto: The mother is killed by the potion and Gretchen becomes pregnant from Faust's visit.

His lust temporarily satisfied, Faust abandons her. He returns much later, only when his passion for her resurfaces, but he has no intention of accepting any responsibility. Clearly the feeling life of Faust is under the control of evil, especially that Luciferic side which gives free rein to emotion and is not lifted by any higher impulse for Good. Upon this return visit, Faust is confronted by Gretchen's brother who is outraged by what has happened to his sister. He draws his sword and duels with Faust; but with the assistance of Mephisto, the brother is slain. Now there is yet another victim of the evil sway which directs Faust's life.

Despite these tragic events there is a turning point late in this Gretchen-portion of the epic. Gretchen is now imprisoned for having drowned the child Faust has fathered. Far off, Faust is part of a satanic, ritual celebration—an annual gathering of demonic figures on Walpurgis Night (April 30). Mephisto has brought him here to complete Faust's total degradation. But in the midst of the celebration, Faust has a vision of the imprisoned Gretchen, and that awakens feelings of compassion and authentic love.

At Faust's insistence, the two of them visit Gretchen in prison. At first they find she has been driven insane by her guilt and the imprisonment. But when Faust demonstrates his sense of grief and care, she responds and is restored to sanity. Now, Faust hopes to help her escape, because she is soon to be executed for the child's murder. But Gretchen refuses to avoid responsibility for her actions. A voice from Heaven announces that she is not condemned but redeemed. By God's grace her immortal soul will be saved after the execution.

Faust and Mephisto depart, and it is evident that Faust has experienced a kind of moral renewal. Despite all the previous manifestations of evil through his life of feeling, a genuine love (which is more than lustful passion) has finally gained the upper hand. Now the assault of Mephisto turns more directly to the *will* of Faust.

Faust, Part II was published many years after Part I, and by Goethe's own choice was made public only after his death. It describes in elaborate images the attack of evil upon the will. Of course, it may be too simplistic to divide the Faust legend into such neat parts. Even in Part I there are issues of choice and will in relation to evil. Just as surely, the assault of evil upon thinking and feeling continues into Part II. (The first portion of Part II concerns a sojourn by Faust into the realms of classical Greece, where his eventual marriage to Helen represents the education and redemption of his feeling life.) However, we can most clearly see Mephisto's efforts to corrupt the will in the last portions of the epic.

Faust has become the man of social action. He has a scheme to build a personal empire of power: He wants to fight the very forces of nature and reclaim from the sea certain lands along the coast. Mephisto suggests a plan to make this possible, which involves helping the Emperor and earning a favor. The Emperor has made some foolish decisions earlier (following Mephisto's financial advice) and now is engaged in a war to defend his throne. But he accepts the offer of Faust and Mephisto for assistance, and, sure enough, Mephisto's invocation of magical forces is enough to win the war for the Emperor. Faust is rewarded with the gift of the coastal land he desires. To this point Faust's project seems laudable—the use of will and determination to create something new in the earth.

However, things begin to change as the project proceeds. Faust's *will to power* expands—he wants control of all the land in the area. There is within him a dark alliance of unrestrained power and shrewd intellect, and it grasps for control of everything. Here we see the Ahrimanic side of evil at work through Mephisto's influence.

One holdout is unwilling, though, to cooperate with Faust's plan. For many years an elderly couple, Philemon and Baucis, have lived in their little cottage and chapel near Faust's palace, and they refuse to sell to him. Their land is original, high ground not reclaimed from the sea. A sharp contrast is drawn between Faust's new world of prosperity and power as opposed to the peasant couple's humble, peaceful way of life. Faust is first annoyed and then haunted by the sounds of their chapel bell. It is a reminder of the spiritual world, an awareness he had once sought with the deepest of conviction. Faust is frustrated because he lacks a spiritual world. He is so caught up in his material possessions and earthly power that he has lost attunement to spiritual reality. His *spiritual* quest has been projected into the *material* world, but in so doing he deceives only himself.

Faust uses his power by willfully moving against this last obstacle to his great design. His fantasy of greatness rules him and contains an element of authoritarianism born of pride and assisted by an obsession for power. He orders Mephisto and his three henchmen to rid him of this problem. His intention is that the couple be moved to a new place, but Mephisto interprets things in his own way and in his roughshod manner the elderly couple is killed—frightened to their deaths. Faust is governor of the region and responsible for the safety of its inhabitants. So, even though he did not order the murders, he knows he is responsible. The forces of evil, working through his will for power, are seemingly in control.

Faust takes upon himself the blame for what has happened and his remorse is genuine. As a consequence of this, he is visited by four gray hags who haunt him; one, named Worry, blinds him.

Near the end of the epic, Faust begins to see the effects of evil on his life and the impact it has had on others. He consciously uses his will to rid himself of demonic forces and to find real freedom. As death approaches, he begins to take his blindness as a blessing and perceives that "within me there beams a radiant light" (line 11,500). He attempts to use his will to act freely and to create a society of free people. This is what at his death he envisions for the future. But Mephisto fails to understand how Faust has redeemed the will, and expects to take Faust's soul at death. To his surprise and dismay, a host of angels comes to carry Faust's body up to Heaven in the final scene.

Building a New Age of Good Will

What are you to do with the opportunity that you face with your life? In what appear to be the smallest of ways, you can make your life a vehicle for *good will* working in the earth. A word of encouragement or hope to someone. A passionate, yet patient, effort to correct an injustice. But to do this noble work you must understand the nature of the other option—the alternative that would misuse the will and fight the purposefulness of life. If you are to be an agent of good will, then you must not be afraid to recognize the reality of evil. That takes careful scrutiny of first yourself and then the world around you. As distasteful as it may seem, as uncomfortable as it may make you, it is required.

To understand evil and how it works is *not* to make you more likely to fall prey to it. To study evil and how it distorts the will is *not* to engage in "negative thinking" or to strengthen its power. You, and everyone like you, who want to work for the Good need to be spiritually grown-up in these troubled times in which we live. The world can ill afford lame or lazy excuses for refusing to see how real are evil and ill-will. It isn't spiritually mature to label the suffering and mistreatment of people at home or abroad as "souls meeting their own karma." In fact, karma may be influential; but a willing spirit which expresses good will sees in the same situation an opportunity to work patiently yet with determination for change.

Nor is it mature to blur all distinctions and pretend that everything is perfect. In a *rush* to experience oneness, many a seeker has prematurely claimed to be there. It is Ahriman himself who tempts us to hurry, to rush to claim something before we have earned it. A oneness—an integration—of the evil urge and the good urge is possible. But it is achieved only by recognizing them both for what they are and not pretending that one is non-existent.

The person who is spiritually mature in his or her seeking can make the difference today. You can be one of them. This is the "Age of the Disordered Will," but there is still hope because a new age is possible. What shall that new age, long promised by so many, look like? It probably won't be recognized by extraordinary breakthroughs of mind—psychic or otherwise. Instead, a credible new age that we can look forward to is the "Age of Good Will." It brings forth a good far beyond what we can now imagine. It has room for the personally empowered individual life *and* for the life which is guided by a Greater Power. It may take 20 years or 2,000 years for such a new epoch to come, but it is your willing spirit that makes it possible.

RECOMMENDED ADDITIONAL READING

Good and Evil, Martin Buber (Scribners, New York, 1952)

This classic book by the eminent Jewish theologian is highly recommended for anyone studying the topic. Buber's sharp, distinct writing allows us to wrestle with some of the deepest paradoxes of good and evil, in ourselves and in the world.

People of the Lie, M. Scott Peck (Simon and Schuster, New York, 1983)

A contemporary study of evil by the psychiatrist who is better known for his book *The Road Less Traveled.* In this second book, however, he deals provocatively with the nature of evil, possession, and the social dimension of evil.

Goethe's View of Evil, Alan Cottrell (Floris Books, Edinburg, Scotland, 1983)

This is a brilliant, deep examination of Goethe's theory of evil, principally as illustrated in his master work *Faust.* Rudolf Steiner was profoundly influenced by Goethe, as is evident from Cottrell's analysis.

CHAPTER NINE

Will, Ideals, and Your Soul's Mission

What is your role in an Age of Good Will? What specific part is yours to play? Perhaps it seems presumptuous to assume that you and every other person have a special calling—a mission or purpose in life. But that is exactly what you can discover with a healthy, balanced will.

The Age of Good Will may be far off or it may be imminent. Paradoxically it is probably both. It may well be *centuries* before the majority of humankind is ready to use free will responsibly and to live as unique individualities. But right *now* you may be ready to make this transition at a personal level. At this very point in your life, you may be prepared to be a co-creator with God—to live consciously for good as a free-willed spirit.

Your soul growth, along the lines of your own destiny for this lifetime, begins with an ideal. In a deeply mysterious way, your encounter with a personal ideal is also a paradox. It is something you select, using your will's power to choose. However, a true, spiritual ideal is also something that chooses you—that reveals itself to you in surprising, wondrous ways. The following simple formula puts it most succinctly:

> Envision your ideal;
>
> Awaken and apply your will;
>
> And soul development is the result.

This brief affirmation summarizes a basic strategy for guiding spiritual development. Although it clearly shows that a proper and healthy use of your will is at the heart of soul growth, the entire approach depends upon a suitable starting point: your personal ideal. In Chapter 5 you completed a training exercise related to the choice of a spiritual ideal, but now it's appropriate to look more closely at this complete subject.

Ideals can be subtle and ambiguous. Much of the confusion arises from the idiomatic meaning the word has assumed in our language. The word "ideal" has strong connotations of unreality and lack of pragmatism. There is a tendency to change the word to the form "idealistic" and to add a prefix, the word "just." To accuse someone of being "just idealistic" is a way of dismissing his or her ideas as (perhaps) admirable but obviously unworkable.

What is needed is a return to a deeper understanding of the original meaning of "ideal." In the Platonic sense, for example, the ideal (or ideal form) exists in a higher dimension and has a more essential and profound reality than what is perceived through the physical senses. In a similar way, it might be said that a significant aspect of your soul's ideal resides in the unconscious and is not immediately accessible to that part of you preoccupied with material life.

Several terms give an accurate feeling for the nature of an ideal. "Life direction" and "purpose" are two of them. Although some people are more immediately aware of this fact than others, we all live our lives with some kind of motivation, which creates a direction of personal development and a sense of purpose in living. For one person, it may be striving for fame; for a second, healing the suffering of humanity; and for yet a third, it might be creative expression. The array of possible motivations is virtually endless, but in each case it reveals the ideal of the individual.

Another word that may shed light on the meaning of ideals is "intentionality," a term sometimes used in theological writings, such as the work of Paul Tillich. In his classic book *Love and Will*, Rollo May builds on Tillich's notions of intentionality and relates it to the healthy functioning of will.

Intentionality encompasses, but is not limited to,

conscious intentions. Your conscious *intention* may be to make a new friend when you strike up a conversation with a stranger, but the broader *intentionality* includes your more fundamental orientation toward humanity in general. That intentionality includes deep currents of motivation and purpose which are largely *unconscious* to you at the moment you start the conversation. In this example, the intentionality (or ideal) may have the quality of oneness and interpersonal connectedness. However, other conscious intentions and intentionalities are equally possible. The immediate intention of starting the conversation could be to remove the boredom of the moment, with little real interest in the other person. In this instance, the intentionality bespeaks a view of other people as objects, to be used to satisfy personal needs.

The example of striking up a conversation with a stranger could include many other conceivable intentions and intentionalities. It is also rather simplistic; life never seems to confront us in quite so elementary a fashion. Nevertheless, the example points out the broader consideration that must be given to studying your own intentionality as opposed to merely your conscious intentions. Ideals (or intentionality) take hold of both conscious and unconscious life. The following three-part model shows levels of the ideal within us: Spiritual Ideal, Incarnation Ideal, and conscious ideal.

The Spiritual Ideal

Within the deepest recesses of your soul is a Spiritual Ideal. It is a "given," an archetype of your spiritual makeup. In this sense the Spiritual Ideal is the same for all souls; rather than being something you have chosen or created, it has been placed within you by the forces of Creation.

The phrase used in the Cayce readings for this Spiritual Ideal is the universal Christ Consciousness. Take note of the use of the word "consciousness" here. An ideal, at any of the three levels which shall be described, is actually a state of consciousness. Since consciousness is created by the interplay of mind and will, there is both a *pattern* quality (i.e., mind) and an *actualizing impetus* (i.e., will) to any

ideal. In this fashion it can be seen that the ideal doesn't
exist independent of the will, but that the first participation
of the will with an ideal is contained *within* the ideal itself.

Although this sounds like an abstract and coldly logical
deduction, take a moment to consider it and feel its
importance. If you mistakenly assume that an ideal is a
phenomenon only of your mind, then do you have much
hope of ever becoming that ideal? Where shall the force of
will come from to make it an actuality? But if you remember
that any ideal is a state of consciousness—that is, a pattern
of mind *and* an impetus of will—then the prospects look
more hopeful. If the ideal is a conscious one, then there
already exists some measure of conscious will to do
something practical with that ideal. If the ideal is more
unconscious (in the same way that intentionality was
presented as having an unconscious flavor), then that will
is an unconscious impetus.*

The first level of the ideal, the Spiritual Ideal, is
unconscious to you. Residing deep within your soul is a
consciousness of the goal of human evolution. The
definition offered in the Cayce readings stresses both its
pattern of mind *and* its will: "the awareness within each
soul, imprinted in pattern on the mind [i.e., the unconscious
mind] and waiting to be awakened by the will, of the soul's
oneness with God." (5749-14) In other words, this Ideal
consciousness is fundamentally one that sees the
interrelationship of all life. But for that pattern of mind to
awaken, the will must be active.

What will do you think is referred to? Most interpreters
of this passage have assumed that it means the conscious
will by which you make efforts to be more spiritual. Such a
line of reasoning concludes that the universal Christ Consciousness is awakened to conscious awareness by
consistently and persistently making efforts with the

*Here again we face a paradox, a seeming contradiction. We use the word
"conscious" to mean a state of consciousness of which we are aware. For
example, as you read this page you are using your conscious will to keep
attention on the words and your conscious mind to analyze their meaning.
But there also exist simultaneously states of consciousness within you of
which you are *not* immediately aware. For the moment, these states of
consciousness constitute your "unconscious" self.

conscious will (meditating daily, eating health foods, keeping one's temper in check, etc.). Such activities no doubt have their place, but is that the whole story?

Re-read the definition above and interpret the word "will" to mean a deep, unconscious will—an impetus toward enlightenment which exists independent of your own efforts. Now the definition takes on new shades of meaning. Now your understanding of the Spiritual Ideal may be altered, so that it no longer looks so remote and inaccessible. The Spiritual Ideal is constantly active. Its impulse is felt most fully within your unconscious self, but it is a will toward your *conscious* enlightenment. This is exactly the discovery made by depth psychologists and psychiatrists like Jung, who have found that there is an impulse toward individuation which seems to have a life (and a will) of its own. The Spiritual Ideal is, therefore, a backdrop against which the next two levels of the ideal operate.

The Incarnation Ideal or Life's Mission

Nothing is more exciting and hopeful than the concept of a personal mission. The chance that your life could have a *specialized purpose* stands in stark contrast to the homogenized, depersonalized and desacralized ways that modern culture operates. Even so-called unique and unusual persons (i.e., the ones celebrated in certain magazines or television programs) in a more subtle way are really "norms" of the culture's value system.

Cayce, Steiner, and Gurdjieff all spoke or wrote of the soul's mission and destiny for a lifetime. Your life's purpose, chosen just before birth, exists as an Incarnation Ideal (or, for short, "Ideal," with the first letter capitalized) within your unconscious self.

In the material called "life readings" given by Cayce, there is presented to individual people not just a fascinating array of past-lifetime scenarios, but more importantly there is counsel regarding the specific purpose for the present lifetime. In the words of one such reading, "...each soul enters with a mission...we all have a mission to perform." (3003-1) That purpose is something broader than merely working on one's own "bad karma." In other words, your mission has a quality of creativity that is life-enhancing and goes beyond just working on your faults.

To appreciate what Cayce's readings are saying about your soul's purpose, recall the distinction made in Chapter 4 between two levels of your being. On the one hand, there is personality—a necessary component to function in the physical world, yet not the more essential you. That ingredient is provided by the individuality or real self. The personality is what you appear to be—your "persona"—or more accurately your array of personae, because the personality is made up of a collection of subpersonalities. It is the nature of your personality to operate by habit, in a rather automatic or reactive way. Sometimes that is helpful, but more often it stifles creativity and individuality.

The individuality is the spiritual "I" which has continuity from lifetime to lifetime. *It is not yet perfected, but it is capable of growth and development.* Whereas the personality functions by habit with little or no real conscious choice, the individuality operates through will. The individuality also has embedded within it the Incarnation Ideal which it selected before birth. That Ideal is to be lived with the personality as its vehicle of expression, but this requires that at least some aspects of the individuality first awaken to conscious life.

The *recognition* of your soul's purpose (or Ideal) is *not* an "all or nothing" thing. In other words, there are degrees of understanding and appreciation. The process unfolds through (1) systematic effort (i.e., use of your conscious will) *in cooperation with* (2) overtures from your deeper self (i.e., the initiatives of your unconscious will). Gradually there is revealed to you the nature of your life's mission. A step-by-step program to make that discovery is described at the end of this chapter.

Your mission in life is something beyond just a professional label like bookkeeper, attorney, or social worker. The Ideal of your soul is to manifest a specific theme of being—a particular way of viewing life, responding to it and creating within it. Again, it should be stressed that your mission is not the repayment of negative karma. Certainly there is reality to limiting karma (i.e., soul memories of having misused physical life opportunities). In fact, the effects of karma must be dealt with and can even block the fulfillment of the real mission. However, your soul's purpose encompasses creative aspects far beyond compensation for past misdeeds.

If your life's purpose isn't exclusively a single occupation, then what is it? Here are examples of thematic statements of a life mission which were proposed to individuals in their own Cayce life readings:

> to be a spiritual leader through the arts

> to demonstrate the spiritual meaning of
> numbers and mathematics

> to be the transmitter and clarifier of ideas

In each of these instances there exists a number of different professional or avocational possibilities (i.e., many souls fulfill a mission more through hobbies or free time interests, than through a career track). You should expect, as well, that at different points in your life span, there will be different ways to give expression to your soul's purpose. What is appropriate at age 35 to serve that Ideal may be quite different from what is best at ages 55 or 75 in serving that same sense of mission. Nevertheless, the Cayce readings present the concept of soul's purpose as something you can start doing at *any* point in a life span. Some people at or near retirement age were told in their life readings what their Incarnation Ideal was, and they were encouraged to work consciously with it, starting immediately.

In a way often similar to Cayce's idea of a soul's mission, Gurdjieff refers to the individual's *destiny*. He uses the term "personality" in an almost identical fashion to the way it is found in the Cayce readings, although he stresses one further feature of its origin. Gurdjieff points out that your personality is largely shaped by what you have taken on or learned through the imitation of other people. The process began in earliest childhood until you now have an acquired side of your self that really is "not you." That personality is made up of many subpersonalities or "I's," each having its own habit patterns and agenda. Some of the "I's" are relatively nice and are useful for functioning in material life. Other "I's" are particularly rigid, narrow-minded or fearful, and they constitute what Gurdjieff calls false personality. Unfortunately your personality, which *could* serve as the instrument or vehicle for expressing your destiny, is typically under the control of your false personality. The practice of honest, objective self-observation (or, "standing aside and watching yourself go by") reveals this fact to you in a less theoretical and far more potent way.

If personality (and its troublesome cousin, false personality) constitute one aspect of your being, what is the other? Cayce uses the term individuality; Gurdjieff calls it "essence" plus the "Real I" which stands behind and can work through essence. "What is truly your own" is essence. When you were a small child, your essence was evident, but it was quickly covered up as you acquired a personality through imitation. But now in your adult life it is possible, through careful and wise work on yourself, to make your personality (especially false personality) more passive or obedient and to make essence more active. In this case, passivity or obedience doesn't mean that you must become a shy, subservient personality in order to contact your essence, but instead that personality and its mechanical reactions to life must have a less assertive control of you.

Your destiny or *fate* (as Gurdjieff often called it) resides within your essence. Real I and Real Will working through essence and manifesting in an obedient personality make the fulfillment of your destiny possible. If you could stay "awake," you would keep in touch with the essence-side of yourself, and therefore with your fate (or destiny). You were born, equipped with the talents and inclinations of your essence, to follow a certain life path. But ordinarily you, like almost everyone else, are out of direct contact with this more authentic self. Influence from personality and false personality takes you in another direction, shaped by imitation of others. In so doing you move out from under the

Law of Fate and operate instead under the Law of Accident, as Gurdjieff called it. Then so much of what you seem to accomplish has little or nothing to do with your real self. You often find yourself in situations that surely may be "karmic" or have a lesson in them; however, these circumstances do not properly belong to your most authentic self and they are not likely to lead you to your destiny.

What is the Law of Fate in contrast to the Law of Accident? The Law of Fate is a principle under which your essence operates. It is "the law of your right destiny," a principle that leads you to situations and people which resonate to the calling which your Real I intends for this lifetime. The implication of "fate" is not that of "fatalism" or "predestination." Instead, it is the predisposition of the soul or Real I for *how* it can *best* develop.

On the other hand, your personality operates by the Law of Accident. The term "accident" is a relative one. Even the events shaped by the Law of Accident can be traced to causes and can provide challenges from which you learn. Those familiar with the axiom, "Nothing happens by chance or accident" (found in the Cayce readings and many other places), need not assume an irreconcilable contradiction here. Gurdjieff would probably admit that the events of typical daily life, directed by personality, do happen with underlying causes. In other words, the personality operating under the Law of Accident can "cause" its own problems and difficulties, or even luck. The question, however, is one of relevancy. Do those causes and behind-the-scenes connections really have anything to do with your own true calling in life? Situations controlled by the Law of Accident are incidental, even irrelevant, to your real destiny.

In other words, if your life is controlled by false personality, then your material life experience is under the Law of Accident. The people and situations you draw to yourself are likely to be the ones you need to fulfill your mission in life. On the other hand, as you learn to reawaken to the essence side of yourself, you come more and more under the Law of Fate, making your soul's purpose for this lifetime a more reachable goal.

Complementing these ideas from Gurdjieff and Cayce about the Incarnation Ideal are statements made by Steiner on the formulation of the soul's destiny for one lifetime. Steiner's teachings provide an elaborate theory of the soul's experience between death and birth, with a description of exact stages which are enacted as the soul draws closer and closer to physical reincarnation. He emphasizes the role played by more highly evolved beings of other realms in helping each soul digest the experience of the last lifetime and prepare for the next. These beings assist in the choice of a plan for the coming lifetime and they help each soul select an appropriate destiny. Then, this pattern is "knit" into the very structure of the higher bodies—the astral and etheric. According to Steiner, there is one last chance to preview the implications of the mission which the soul has chosen. The Anthroposophical scholar Stewart Easton summarizes Steiner's clairvoyant view of this process by writing:

> While still in the moon sphere and just as we are forming our etheric body, we have one last overwhelming experience that corresponds exactly to the tableau that passed before our vision after death while the etheric body was dissolving. This time, however, we have a prevision of the earthly life that faces us, not in all its details as in the vision after death, but in its general outline. This is the life we have planned for ourselves, including all the compensations for former wrongs that we now intend to right, and perhaps great but painful deeds that we intend to perform for the sake of humanity and future lives on earth. (*Man and World in the Light of Anthroposophy*, p. 165)

But even with these purposeful patterns built into the bodies of the soul, the details of life experience are not predetermined. Destiny can work in wondrous ways to bring you into contact with promising opportunities, in the form of people or situations. But thereafter it is a matter of your choice and free will. Easton adds, ". . . at the moment we meet someone with whom we are linked the element of destiny is at an end, and we are from that time onward on our own." (p. 157)

The Conscious Ideal

The *conscious* spiritual ideal is the third level at which the concept of an ideal is useful. As the term implies, the conscious ideal is your best, current understanding of what your life is about. Admittedly a narrow, fear-based orientation to life may produce a conscious ideal which is self-serving (e.g., fame or greed). However, anyone who has seriously considered that life has both physical *and* spiritual dimensions is likely to set a conscious ideal with spiritual overtones.

In Training Exercise #11 of Chapter 5, you chose a word or phrase to represent your spiritual ideal. It is a statement of personal aspiration. But it may also be a reminder of something you have already experienced, however briefly. It is an aspiration because the spiritual ideal calls you to be the self you rarely remember to be. At its best, it is also the recollection of personal experience because, without having had at least a fleeting taste of that different identity, the spiritual ideal remains a dry, theoretical concept in your life.

The notion of your spiritual ideal rooted in actual, personal experiences cannot be stressed too much. Certainly, it is fine to have hopes related also to things beyond the scope of personal experience. You may trust the words of others more advanced along the spiritual path than you are and have faith that some day you too will have similar experiences. No doubt, this kind of aspiration and hope is a powerful influence for spiritual growth. But the conscious spiritual ideal is best understood as something different from this kind of faith.

Something special takes place when you identify experiences from your past which have had a spiritually quickening effect upon you. When you choose a spiritual ideal which is related to a taste or glimpse that you have actually received of your individuality/essence/Real I, then there is no room for doubt about its reality. Admittedly, you may have questions about your capacity to sustain that sense of personal identity, but it is not a matter of doubting that that place in consciousness exists. Because you know so clearly and so personally that this spiritual ideal is authentic, you can at any moment use your will to call it back to mind, *unfettered by doubt about its reality.*

A spiritual ideal which is rooted in personal experience also allows you to avoid another pitfall in setting ideals. If you are like most others, there is a tendency to set your spiritual ideal in terms of the "shoulds" and "oughts" of key authority figures in your life, even spiritual authority figures. Something deeper within your soul, however, will not feel comfortable with this. It will rebel if your spiritual ideal is set in terms of what your parents or schoolteachers or church leaders have said your ideals ought to be. Actually it is a shortcut produced by your own personality to set a spiritual ideal in such a manner. Remember that your personality is largely the product of what you have taken on from other people. It tends to suggest a spiritual ideal made up of such "shoulds" and "oughts" which come from others. In fact, to allow your life to be guided by a spiritual ideal which has been determined in that way serves only to perpetuate the current form of your life.

Instead, your spiritual ideal is best chosen as a sense of personal identity that is uniquely you. Beyond habit and routine, it descibes a place of clarity from which you are free to create and live your mission. A spiritual ideal, in the fullness of its potential for power, may have a vision-ary/revelatory quality to it. In other words, it is based on experiences of yourself, however brief or long ago, in which a vision of who you really are was revealed to you. For some people, the vision was vague and fuzzy, but different enough from the typical way of knowing oneself that there was obviously something special about it. For other people, the revelation was extraordinarily distinct and over-whelming in its impact.

Such a "vision" or "revelation" has *not* come for most people as an ethereal, hallucinatory experience. More often these moments have come in a quieter way in the midst of daily living. But they are always received with an element of surprise. They come unexpectedly, bringing a sense of wonder. In fact, they often leave your personality self feeling uncomfortable, because your individuality self usually sees life in quite a different way.

Take a moment to look back and see the word or phrase you previously selected as a spiritual ideal—i.e., your results for Training Exercise #11 in Chapter 5. Then, try again to choose the best possible wording for your ideal, this time using the following series of questions and instructions:

Can you recall any peak spiritual moments? Are there key experiences from your past that are still profoundly influential in your spiritual quest? Are there times when you tasted or caught a glimpse of a more authentic way of knowing yourself?

Drawing largely upon these important memories, set a spiritual ideal for your life. Give your individuality/essence/Real I identity a label by choosing a descriptive word or phrase for this place inside yourself. Don't be concerned if the words you select do not sound lofty enough. What matters is that they are personally meaningful. Your spiritual ideal is something so real to you that there is no room to doubt it, even though you lack the capacity to be in touch with it all the time.

Your conscious ideal is likely to alter as you grow spiritually. That is to say, your understanding of the best label for your individuality may change. It is not a matter of the Ideal of your soul for this lifetime changing, but rather your vision and understanding of it can become clearer.

In Gurdjieff's system the concept of *aim* closely corresponds to the conscious ideal presented in Cayce's readings. A genuine, effective conscious ideal is more than just a superficial, lofty aspiration. It does not merely say "ought" or "should," nor does it come from the intellect alone. In a similar way Gurdjieff presents real aim as something deeply experienced and emotionally felt.

Real aim begins by self-observation and the recognition of something in yourself to be transformed. Real aim intends to take recurrent life events and find new reactions to them instead of the rigid, automatic responses of false personality. Have you been using your will regularly to practice self-observation? Based on what you have objectively observed about yourself, are you ready to formulate a real aim in your conscious life?

If so, then do not assume that such an aim shall be easily accomplished. Your efforts to set and follow it are like the intention to sail across the ocean from America to Europe. It is rarely possible to follow a direct course because of the changing currents and winds of life. Sailing often requires "tacking" or going along pathways diagonal to the eventual goal—a kind of flexibility and adaptability which never loses sight of the final destination. But when conscious ideals or aims are consistent with the deeper Ideal, then soul growth is possible—the development of your more essential, real self can happen.

How to Discover Your Soul's Purpose

Step 1: Set Your Ideal. Once you have set your conscious spiritual ideal, you have taken the first step toward identifying your mission for this lifetime. That spiritual ideal is your best, current understanding of the nature of your own individuality and its Ideal for this incarnation. However, in order to clarify the specific direction of that mission, a deeper search is needed.

How can you find the exact nature of your soul's purpose? One approach is to ask a psychically sensitive person to attempt to "read" your unconscious life and identify the nature of your mission. The problems with this approach are (1) finding a reliable psychic and (2) evaluating what the psychic tells you. Another approach is to conduct a personal research project—an experiment with specific steps like those described in this chapter. But whatever approach you use, the mission statement you arrive at should be measured by these two questions:

Does the stated purpose of my life ring true, does it strike a chord in my intuitive, feeling self?

Does the stated purpose show fruits when I start trying to apply it?

What kind of "fruits" might you expect to see when you start applying your true mission in life? There are five signposts or indicators of things to watch for. They are reinforcements to show that you are on track with your soul's purpose.

(1) A deeper sense of *wonder*. Living your soul's purpose creates a feeling of life expanding and opening up before you, with surprise and awe. You feel the magical quality to life.

(2) *Others benefit* as you creatively contribute to the world through some form of service. Sometimes the act of service and the benefit to others are quite direct (e.g., one of the so-called "helping professions," such as nursing, counseling, etc.). In other instances, the service may be just as real yet indirect (e.g., an artist whose creations later uplift and inspire others).

(3) Feeling a greater *closeness to God*. Of course, *how* to recognize this is an ancient question. But, if God is understood as completeness and wholeness, then you can expect to experience the Presence as that which makes you more whole. So, begin by recognizing how you are not yet whole. What do you most deeply feel is missing in your life? For example, if you feel in darkness (i.e., confused) then greater closeness to God shall be experienced as light or profound understanding. If you feel trapped or limited, then God's Presence shall be felt as freedom. If you have been caught in a great loneliness, then God can especially be experienced as intimate companionship and support.

(4) Seeing *purposefulness in all of life*. As you live your soul's purpose, it simultaneously awakens you to the recognition of purpose in the lives of others. You begin to be sensitive to the underlying reasons and opportunities inherent in life events all around you. Such a sensitivity may assist you in efforts to help other people consciously understand their missions in life.

(5) A *joyful attitude* toward living. Perhaps the most evident characteristic of a person who is living his or her mission in life is joy. It may manifest as a bubbly, extroverted enthusiasm for life. Or, in other individuals, it may express in a quieter way. But, in whatever form it

expresses through you, joy is the hallmark of a life which is fulfilling its Ideal.

Step 2: Identify Your Soul's Assets. Having already decided on a word or phrase for your conscious spiritual ideal, you are ready to identify your talents, strengths, abilities, and aptitudes. The Cayce life readings most often did this in astrological terms and past-lifetime scenarios. However, any serious and honest self-appraisal is likely to provide you with a similar kind of list. What works best is to identify between eight and ten especially significant talents and abilities which you know are within you. Some of them are ones you are already using in life (but perhaps not with as deep a sense of fulfillment as you know is possible). Other talents you put on your list may be ones that you rarely, if ever, get a chance to use, yet you know that ability is accessible to you. Here is a list of sample talents and abilities which other people have recognized in themselves. It may help you get started on identifying your own.

friendly	sense of humor
innovative	articulate
sensitive	forgiving
creative	orderly
imaginative	kind
trouble-shooter	patient
good with animals	listening
good with plants	cooperative
good with children	playful nature
good with _____	logical
energetic	motivator
psychic	financially adept
writing	loyal
decisive	artistic
empathetic	mechanically skilled
leadership	intuitive
practical	industrious
good cook	planning
wise	committed
teaching	musical

But before completing your list of talents, consider one additional approach for finding soul strengths. Some of your most significant abilities may lie hidden in your faults and weaknesses. Using Stage 2 will—skillful will—you can find a new orientation for some personal characteristics which you have always labeled as faults. You may find a seed of great strength or talent within a weakness.

For example, suppose that two of your personality faults are impatience and stubbornness. Buried within your tendency to be impatient might be a deep commitment to have things done right. This important strength of your soul may be twisted and misunderstood so that it comes out looking like impatience. Although the weakness still needs to be changed, this seed of something good should be recognized. In a similar fashion, the fault of stubbornness may contain at its heart the quality of persistence. However, when persistence is mixed with misunderstanding or fear, the result can be a fault like stubbornness. Nevertheless, this soul talent for persistence may have a key role to play in your life's mission.

Make a list of three or four of your most noticeable personality faults. Now, one by one look at each weakness with new eyes. Can you find the seed of something good in that fault—perhaps a strength or talent which has become distorted? You may not immediately find something for every fault. But if you identify a hidden talent or strength in this way, add it to your list of soul strengths.

What you now have is a list of about eight to twelve talents and abilities you know are within you. Think of this as your list of candidates. All of them may have a role to play in *living* your soul's purpose, but a smaller number of them are crucial for *identifying* what that purpose is. From the total of candidates, you will narrow the list down to about four or five which are most significant.

For example, suppose that your initial inventory yields a candidate list of a dozen talents and strengths. Eight of them are ones you at least occasionally use in daily life; two are talents you know you have within you, although they are rarely—if ever—used; and two are strengths which exist like seeds within your personality faults. For most people, the basic features of the soul's purpose are shaped by only four or five particularly important talents. All strengths and talents are probably used in some *supportive* role, but you can expect that about *four or five* abilities will be most significant in *defining* that mission.

The question remains, "How do you narrow the longer candidate list down to this smaller number?" In the example above, how would you pick the most important four or five from the original list of twelve? You can pose two questions to yourself that should help in this selection process:

(1)Which of these talents and strengths seem to be right at the core of your real self, your best self? That is to say, some of the talents and strengths on your candidate list will be recognizable as belonging to your essence. It would be hard for you to imagine being yourself without them. They are probably ones which began showing up in your childhood or adolescence.

On the other hand, some of the talents and strengths on your candidate list may belong to your personality—to your "acquired, imitative" self. Those talents and strengths have the "inner taste" or "inner feeling" of your having copied them from people you respect and admire. Even these acquired talents may have a helpful role to play in *living* your soul's purpose. But the first group—the talents and strengths of your essence—is most important in *identifying* the exact nature of that mission.

(2) Which talents give you the feeling that there are some additional ways that you can make use of them in order to be really fulfilled? In other words, which strengths on your inventory list seem to speak to you saying, "There is more that you are supposed to be doing with me," even if you have no idea as yet what that "something more" is.

You are ready to move on to Step 3 when you have made a tentative list of the four or five talents which you suspect are the key ones shaping your mission.

Step 3: Formulate a Mission Theme. The next step requires great intuition, imagination, and creative insight about your life. It also requires a willingness on your part to playfully adopt the role of a researcher. In this step you identify a tentative or hypothetical wording for your mission. It is only a likely possibility because confirmation awaits testing and application. Like any type of research there is an element of trial and error—an educated best guess which still needs to be tried out. Your "guess" of a thematic wording for your soul's purpose can be a highly insightful and even inspired one, but it still requires application and testing in daily life for validation.

It is possible, of course, to formulate an erroneous wording for your mission at this step. You may pick something that looks right, only to find in Steps 4 and 5 that things don't go right. Then, like any good researcher, you shall need to come back to Step 3 and try again. If you are fortunate, then your first, tentative wording for your mission may show good fruits when you put it into application. But if not, try to keep in mind how many of the great inventions of history (e.g., the electric light bulb) were developed by researchers who tested many mistaken hypotheses before hitting on the right one.

There are three exercises you are encouraged to complete in working on Step 3. Each one is designed to give you further clues, hints or pieces of the puzzle. One or two may be more helpful to you than another, and you can certainly complete them in whatever order you prefer. But each is designed to help you move from a point where you have a conscious spiritual ideal plus a short list of key talents to the point where you formulate a tentative thematic wording of your soul's mission.

Exercise #1 is a life review of special moments. Take ten or fifteen minutes of relaxed, quiet time to complete an unhurried review of your life. You may want to put on some soft meditation music to help you get into a reverie state. During your life review, look for times in your past when you did things which created strong feelings of "*this* is what I'm supposed to be doing in life—this is the real me coming through." Those moments may have happened years ago or very recently. They may have involved trying something out of the ordinary for you, *or* doing something familiar but in a new way or with a new attitude. During the reverie, as you recall one or more of these moments in your past, it is just as important to note *why* or *how* you were doing something, as it is *what* you were doing. Those specific memories may not tell you exactly what your life's mission is, but they may provide some helpful clues.

Exercise #2 is to re-examine your list of four or five talents. Take another look at your strengths and ask yourself these two questions: As a group, do they seem to point in any direction? Do they suggest a particular kind of service to the world or a creative way of living? Just by examining your list of most significant soul strengths you may get a clue as to the nature of your mission. Think of those talents as a *team*. What is that team especially well suited to do? You may be able to get some additional insight from this exercise by doing it with a friend who knows you well. With such a person, share your brief list of key strengths and ask that person what kind of life mission he or she sees as one which would draw upon those abilities.

Exercise #3 is to consider a list of *example* mission themes. The following list of sample statements of soul's purpose may prove to be helpful to you in creating a thematic wording for your own. Many of them are drawn from counsel given in Edgar Cayce's life readings. Others are taken from the self-exploration of individuals like you who were using these steps to find their own mission. Notice that the examples do not list professional labels like housekeeper, hair stylist, airline pilot, etc. Instead, each one gives a thematic description of a certain quality of consciousness or type of service to be done in the world. For each example, many possible occupations or hobbies might be considered as ways to put the mission into practical application.

Don't rush through this exercise. It is very important to invest some time in thinking about these sample mission themes. Take at least a minute to consider each one of these examples, and for each one ask yourself:

Are there times in my life when I've lived with that sense

of purpose, even for a brief period?

If so, what were the inner and outer results of those efforts?

Do I "resonate" to this theme? Does it feel right? Does it provide a good "fit" with the talents and strengths I have?

Could I adapt the wording of this example theme into something resembling it but more suited to me? Or, can I combine this example with another one?

Here are now some sample mission themes:

awakener of faith
agent of inner and outer peace
healer of minds
humble servant
to cooperate with Spirit in nature
catalyst for change and growth
innovator—the one who gets new things started
transmitter and clarifier of ideas
sensitive, receptive listener who hears the souls of others
motivator and helper of the undeveloped and immature to come to blossom
to bring hope to others
spiritual inspirer through _____ (e.g., the arts, words, numbers/geometry)
finisher—one who brings things to a completion
to appreciate and reflect beauty
discerning, wise analyst of life
celebrator—channel of joyous play
to synthesize, blend, and unify the fragments of life
to keep things pure
worker for justice
balancer—one who keeps things harmonious
spokesperson for truth
to manifest God's love through the family
to show compassion for those less fortunate
healer of bodies
attractor and channel for material supply
magnifier of ideals and aspirations

After you have completed this third exercise and the previous two, it is time to decide upon a tentative theme for your life's purpose—a best, current guess with which you are willing to experiment further. But this is no wild guess or shot in the dark. Using both common sense and intuition, the tentative theme you select has a good chance of proving to be exactly what your soul intends for this lifetime.

Before arriving at your decision, you may want to include prayer, meditation, and dreams for guidance. Up until now in this discovery process, you have been making decisions with your conscious will. It may be time to listen for the promptings of a higher will. A strong feeling at the end of prayer and meditation may steer you in a certain direction as you decide upon tentative wording for your mission. Or, a dream may come in response to all your conscious efforts—a dream that reveals more of your soul's intentions, which have long been unconscious to you.

Step 4: List Applications of the Mission Theme. This step involves brainstorming for practical, new ways to express your mission statement. The focus is to make the best possible use of your key talents and strengths. One by one you can reconsider the four or five talents you chose for Step 2. What are the ways in which you could start using each talent in service to that mission?

For this step there are two categories of practical applications you should list. First: How can you use your talents and fulfill your mission by reaching out to *other people*? Second: How can you use those same strengths and live your soul's purpose by helping *yourself*? In other words, it's *not* selfish to invest time, energy, and talents in your own growth. In fact, it is one part of your soul's mission.

For Step 4 you can probably get the best results by writing down just two or three applications for one category (i.e., reaching out to others) and two or three for the second category (i.e., helping yourself). Sometimes a friend or family member can be of assistance at Step 4— brainstorming with you the many possibilities. But then it's up to you to select just a few on which to work. Keep them practical and specific. The example below of Margaret illustrates a good approach.

Step 5: Test Out the Application in Actual Life. It may not be effective to try all your new applications at once. Pace yourself. Find a way to test the various new expressions as you reasonably have the time and opportunity. It involves an act of will, but a patient, persistent will.

Watch for some or all of the five reinforcing signs that show you are on the right track: (1) feeling the wonder and magic of life, (2) seeing others benefited, (3) knowing more directly the Presence of God, (4) recognizing the purposefulness in all life, and (5) feeling joy. Some of the signs may happen more dramatically for you than others. But if none of these signs occurs, go back to Step #3 and formulate a different mission theme.

An Example of Finding Your Life's Mission

The story of Margaret makes clearer the procedure involved in all these steps. She was a 41-year-old homemaker at the time she started working with this personal research project to find her soul's purpose. She had married at age 22 right after graduation from college with a degree in art. Soon after her marriage, she and her husband started their family, and Margaret had not worked outside the home since the birth of their children 16 and 14 years ago.

Feeling that her life was at a turning point, she started this discovery process by working on her ideals. After considerable self-study, she arrived at a wording for her conscious spiritual ideal: centered and hopeful compassion. Although this gave her a way of naming that place within herself called individuality, it did not yet tell her clearly what her mission in life was. Something more focused and applicable was necessary. *How* was she to go about living that ideal? What were her most important strengths? For what activities did these soul talents especially suit her?

Her next step was to create an inventory of her strengths, a list that turned out to have eleven entries. From that larger list she narrowed it down to four talents that had the feeling of greatest significance for her: artistic, optimistic, idealistic, sensitive to feelings. Interestingly, one of her key talents was a strength embedded in a personality fault. By her own admission Margaret was a dreamer, often coming up with schemes that had no hope of realization. Yet upon careful scrutiny, she saw that the essential seed within that weakness was a fierce idealism.

After completing the three exercises designed to help her arrive at a tentative wording for her mission, she selected this thematic phrase: to be the magnifier of aspirations and ideals. By those words she meant the work of recognizing and enhancing the highest calling in herself and others. She felt that it was her mission to assist people to believe in and trust those quiet, deep aspirations of the soul that so easily get ignored or explained away.

To test the validity of this hypothesis, she wrote down half a dozen practical applications she could start testing. Each practical application was a way she could imagine giving life to her mission.

Some of the applications to test involved direct service to others. For example, using her artistic strength, she resolved to (1) seek a part-time art therapy job and (2) start encouraging more family artistic activities. Her intuition was that art is one way in which people's aspirations and ideals can surface. To better use her talent for sensitivity to feelings, she resolved to test a way of planning her daily life so that it left more time just to be with people and listen to them, instead of always being in a rush. She was willing to test the possibility that if she made more room in her life for people, she would see opportunities to help them magnify their aspirations.

Some of her applications for testing, however, did not focus overtly on service to others. Some involved further development of a key talent. For example, she decided to sign up for a counseling course at the local college. She hoped that a structured attempt to improve her natural sensitivity to others would better equip her to serve.

Just as important, some of her planned experiments involved service to herself—the nurturance of her individuality. She knew it was important for anyone embarking on this discovery to keep that option in mind. If *everything* she wrote down as a practical expression of her soul's purpose was an act of self-sacrificing service, then it would be easy to end up with burnout. Surely some features of living her mission included using key talents to nurture her own best self.

With this principle in mind, Margaret resolved to keep a weekly time for her own creative art work, with special focus on letting her art give form to her ideals. This particular experimental application is an example of blending two talents into one commitment. In addition, she planned to use her soul strength of optimism to nurture her individuality identity. She planned to make it a discipline to believe in herself more deeply—regularly to affirm confidence in herself for meeting difficulties and challenges with creativity and love. She clearly saw that in the long run she would never be very effective as a magnifier of aspirations in others if she didn't use her strength of optimism in relation to herself.

The final step in the process for Margaret was to start testing these applications. Some could be put to use immediately. Others, like the search for a part-time art therapy job, took longer. As she applied and tested them, she looked for several things. As a researcher, she was seeking confirming, validating signs and remained alert to them.

One kind of evidence was a natural and unfolding *flow* to the efforts. Many verbal expressions capture this subtle feeling of life, and they all point to a certain intuitive rightness to what you are doing: "everything fell into place," or "being at the right place at the right time," or "finding that what's needed is provided." Of course, this doesn't mean that there are no problems or difficulties. Living your mission in life shall surely involve being stretched and challenged. But mingled in with the difficulties, you can expect to find reinforcing encouragement *when* you are on track with living your soul's purpose.

For example, at first Margaret couldn't find any part-time art therapy job. But rather than take this as an immediate sign that she was on the wrong track, she decided to take it just one more step before concluding that her hypothesis was in error. She volunteered to teach bi-weekly art classes at a nearby retirement community. Here "things fell into place" and began to unfold as if they had a life of their own. She experienced herself actually magnifying the best aspirations of people as she helped members of that community give their own (admittedly amateurish) expression to ideals through art. Eventually she created a paying part-time job for herself because her volunteer work was so well received.

Of course, not every application to be tested turned out with successful results. One experiment made use of her talent for optimism. She offered to teach the high schoolers' class in Sunday school at her church. She had always seen this group as full of cynicism and sarcasm, resulting from their self-doubts and low self-esteem. This application of her soul's purpose seemed like a natural. What a great chance to help others to magnify their ideals. She was given the job, but unfortunately she had a frustrating experience with it. She didn't give up easily, but was finally forced to conclude that for this time in her life, it was not a service situation that fit her soul's abilities and intentions. The discouraging results with this part of the experiment did *not*, however, invalidate the hypothesis that her soul's mission was "to be the magnifier of ideals and aspirations." Validating feedback came to her through the other applications she tested. But this "failure" did show her at least one parameter of her mission—it showed one point of limitation, at least for now.

Perhaps the *most* significant result of her testing period was the fact that certain qualities of life became more and more frequent experiences for her. In Margaret's case it was a greater sense of joy, a deeper feeling of the wonder of life and a more frequent feeling of the presence of God. These features are among the five reinforcing signs previously described. More than anything else, the occurrence of these indicators convinced her that she had accurately chosen a thematic wording for her soul's mission.

But what if those reinforcing signs did *not* become a more

frequent experience? What if the testing of her various applications had been accompanied by flatness, ordinariness or boredom? Or, what if virtually none of her applications created a natural flow to suggest the rightness of her efforts? Then, as a researcher, she would have been forced to conclude that her hypothesis was in error. She would have had to return to an earlier step and repeat it in a new way—probably to Step 3: selecting another wording for her soul's purpose.

With sincerity and persistence anyone can find his or her mission for this lifetime. If you are fortunate, you may have to go through the sequence of steps only once. But if you meet with initial failure or a mistaken notion, then a repetition of some previous steps is required. However, no investment of time, energy, and effort is more worthwhile than this discovery process. The sense of meaning in life and the possibility of fulfillment it offers are the greatest gifts you can present to yourself.

Summary of the Will's Role

Finding and living your soul's purpose is impossible without your will. In fact, your will participated in the creation of your Incarnation Ideal. That level of will, now largely unconscious to you, is nevertheless still active as it nudges you with feelings and intuitions toward a more purposeful life.

But your conscious will has an important role to play, too. The awakening of a healthy, balanced will strengthens your identity as individuality. It makes it possible to disidentify from habitual personality—to "stand aside and watch self go by." Through this kind of self-observation exercise, you can recognize the automatic, mechanical patterns of your personality which can block you from fulfilling your mission. Even when you feel that you have successfully identified the nature of your soul's purpose, this self-observation work must be maintained. There is always the temptation to fall back "asleep" and to live under the control of habitual, familiar personality.

Most important, your will is the crucial ingredient to the application of your mission. First, it makes possible the practical testing of your "best guess" at the wording for your mission. No amount of intellectual effort can ever validate what you only suspect to be your soul's purpose. Genuine confidence in having correctly discerned your mission comes only from having started to practice it in physical life situations. Your will is what makes that confirmation possible.

Second, your will is the crucial ingredient for applying your soul's purpose because it alone can provide the persistence, determination, discipline, and courage required to fulfill the mission. It alone allows you to meet the challenges and difficulties sure to arise over the years as you manifest what you were destined to do this lifetime. In other words, you as a soul have *chosen* something very special to create and contribute to the world. It is something that shall stretch you and require the deepest kind of commitment. But it is do-able; it can be accomplished. Your will is your greatest ally in living your soul's purpose.

RECOMMENDED ADDITIONAL READING

Spiritual Pilgrims, John Welch (Paulist Press, New York, 1982)

Jungian psychology has deep respect for the idea that healthy ego development should precede explorations into the transpersonal realm. The author is a Carmelite priest who has made an extraordinary synthesis of the writings of Jung and a fellow Carmelite who lived some 400 years ago, the mystic Teresa of Avila. He uses the basic notions from Jung of individuation and archetypes to draw parallels with Teresa's stages of the inner spiritual journey. It is fascinating reading, full of practical applications for any seeker, and also provides one of the best summaries of Jungian thought.

Memories, Dreams, Reflections, Carl G. Jung (Vintage Books, New York, 1961)

This fine, readable autobiography was written near the end of his life. It provides a beautiful narrative and "case history" of Jung's own life as an example of the individuation process.

Discovering Your Soul's Purpose, Mark Thurston (A.R.E. Press, Virginia Beach, Va., 1984)

A more in-depth explanation of this topic, which includes a chapter on reincarnation and two chapters on the will.

Lost Christianity, Jacob Needleman (Doubleday, Garden City, N.Y., 1980)

Although the will is rarely discussed overtly in this book, the principle of "directed attention" is a key ingredient. The premise of Dr. Needleman's inquiry is that a lost or "esoteric" approach to Christianity is not so much a set of hidden facts about metaphysical or mystical life, but instead an intermediate stage of spiritual development. This intermediate or esoteric Christianity has as its purpose the building of a conscious soul, that which can stand between spirit and matter and be the bridge. This is an engrossing, deep book that may radically alter your notions of Christianity. It reads somewhat like a philosophical mystery story as Needleman travels around the world in search of a lost tradition in Christian spirituality.

To Live Again, Catherine Marshall (McGraw-Hill, New York, 1957)

Chapter 4 is a remarkable personal example of one individual finding her mission in life. She even expresses it as a succinct, thematic statment.

What Color Is Your Parachute? Richard Nelson Bolles (Ten Speed Press, Berkeley, Calif., 1986)

This book is focused principally on how to get the right job for you. It is updated yearly to keep the facts fresh. Many of the self-analysis techniques may be helpful to you, in addition to the nuts and bolts of how to find a job that fits your own sense of personal mission.

The Power of a Willing Spirit

We are citizens of a Disordered Age. No doubt, people of every generation have felt that way, but we can lay special claim to the distinction. First, we live in times of unprecedented change—scientific, ethical, political, and social, to name just a few. A sense of disorder is inevitable when old ways die out and new ways emerge. But second, and more important, ours is a Disordered Age because we have become so confused about the nature of *power*.

To move out of this Disordered Age, we need to reconnect with a more authentic meaning for power. Not coercion. Not money. Not destructive ability. The genuine meaning of power comes only from an encounter with the sacred. But we have largely lost touch with a feeling of the sacred. Compared to previous times throughout human history, we in the Western, technological world are missing something profound. We lack a personal relationship with the magical, awe-inspiring side of life. Our rituals, which used to provide this encounter, seem empty to most people today. What modern rituals can we create together to re-establish this connection? How can we find new ways of being nurtured and fed by a higher Power?

Of course, we suspect that a relationship with the sacred is possible, because we have caught glimpses that it is there. Haven't we all had a taste of the sacred and of what it can teach us about the real meaning of power? These extraordinary peak moments of life are filled with wonder.

How have they happened for you? Maybe your list would include things like this: reading a poem that made you cry; the first time you flew in an airplane; a first kiss; a marriage; the birth of a child.

What are those events? They are moments of *presence* to ourselves—our authentic selves—and to something universal. They are moments of amazing personal empowerment *simultaneous* with the most profound humility and surrender. What magic they convey! Yet what a bewildering paradox they reveal! Our encounters with the sacred remind us that there are two sides of power that must be balanced if either is to have any lasting value. On the one hand is power growing out of a healthy personal will. On the other hand is a greater power flowing from a Higher Will. Yet they need each other—neither by itself gives genuine meaning to human life.

To balance the two sides of power does *not* mean a "50-50 split." It's not a juggling act like the one we may try to use when "balancing" a home life and a career. Instead, the paradox of power requires a delicate synthesis in which the two sides can be present together.

Such a rare accomplishment comes only if you are *willing* to stand a certain creative, spiritual tension in your life. What does it feel like? Things cannot be cut-and-dried. Yet decisions are made. There is ambiguity, but it is not confusion. There is a humble feeling about the unresolvable question that comes from being human. There is also the deepest respect for the mystery of life.

The spiritual search is essentially one of balancing personal will and Higher Will. At the same time, the real meaning of power lies in that same wise synthesis of two realms. It requires a kind of will—a kind of power and presence to ourselves—which the world has rarely seen. Yet this is exactly what the human family now so desperately needs. This book has attempted to show some of the ways you can get started. You can be among those leaders who move out of the Disordered Age into an Age of Good Will.

Will-Training Exercises

Exercises	Date Started	Experiences and Results
1. Meditation		
2. Small group work		
3. Self-observation		
4. Disciplines countering habits		
5. Loving self-assertion		
6. Staying in the now		
7. Positive imitation		
8. Building rhythms		
9. Letting go of mechanization		
10. Purposeful body movement		
11. Choosing a spiritual ideal		
12. Setting a reachable goal daily		

INDEX

THE WORK OF EDGAR CAYCE TODAY

The Association for Research and Enlightenment, Inc. (A.R.E.®), is a membership organization founded by Edgar Cayce in 1931.

• 14,145 Cayce readings, the largest body of documented psychic information anywhere in the world, are housed in the A.R.E. Library/Conference Center in Virginia Beach, Virginia. These readings have been indexed under 10,000 different topics and are open to the public.

• An attractive package of membership benefits is available for modest yearly dues. Benefits include: a bi-monthly magazine; lessons for home study; a lending library through the mail, which offers collections of the actual readings as well as one of the world's best parapsychological book collections, names of doctors or health care professionals in your area.

• As an organization on the leading edge in exciting new fields, A.R.E. presents a selection of publications and seminars by prominent authorities in the fields covered, exploring such areas as parapsychology, dreams, meditation, world religions, holistic health, reincarnation and life after death, and personal growth.

• The unique path to personal growth outlined in the Cayce readings is developed through a worldwide program of study groups. These informal groups meet weekly in private homes.

• A.R.E. maintains a visitors' center where a bookstore, exhibits, classes, a movie, and audiovisual presentations introduce inquirers to concepts from the Cayce readings.

• A.R.E. conducts research into the helpfulness of both the medical and nonmedical readings, often giving members the opportunity to participate in the studies.

For more information and a color brochure, write or phone:

A.R.E., P.O. Box 595
Virginia Beach, VA 23451, (804) 428-3588